To the Memory of

Those Who Fell in the Battle of Bristol

Illustrations by

BERYL THORNBOROUGH

BRISTOL SIREN NIGHTS

DIARIES AND STORIES
OF THE BLITZES

VIRTUTE ET INDUSTRIA

Compiled by
The Rev. S. PAUL SHIPLEY

REDCLIFFE
Bristol

First published in 1944 by Rankin Brothers Ltd
First republished by Redcliffe Press Ltd in 1989

ISBN 0 948265 98 1

Printed and Bound by WBC, Bristol

FOREWORD

By the BISHOP OF BRISTOL.

It was a happy thought which inspired Mr. Shipley to compile this collection of human documents, describing the raids from which Bristol suffered in the winter of 1940/41, and the splendid way in which its citizens stood up to them. I venture to prophesy that in days to come his book will be read and re-read, both by those who experienced the horror of the " blitzes," and by their children.

The chief impression made by this record of courage, endurance and cheerfulness in face of danger is that the spirit of man is unconquerable. That is a truth we shall do well to remember when we are faced by dangers and anxieties of a different kind, but making as great demands upon our fortitude.

This story of the air-raids will help us to remember, and Bristolians will be grateful to Mr. Shipley for the book which he has given them.

THE BISHOP'S STORY

In a seriously damaged street in East Bristol a piece of paper was pinned on the door of a partly ruined house with these words in a child's handwriting: " They helped every one his neighbour; and every one said to his brother, Be of good courage." (Isaiah xli. 6.)

INTRODUCTION

This book has been written by Bristol people for Bristol people, but I hope it will circulate far and wide so that others may be inspired by the way Bristolians " took it."

It originated from a suggestion made at a meeting of the Bath and Bristol Writers' Circle that someone should collect into a volume stories of the blitzes on our city, thus giving them a permanent home. This book is the result! In these pages I have gathered together as many of these stories as I could come by. All of them are authentic, and some have an historic interest.

No such book as this could claim to be complete, for there must be many stories of heroism, pathos and humour which will for ever remain untold. But from those related here the citizens of to-morrow will be able to visualise how we of this generation faced up to the Luftwaffe during the dark days of 1940-41.

Never in her history of a thousand years has Bristol had such a fiery trial. She was right on the front line during that winter and spring. In a few hours the memorials of centuries were swept away, and the face of the city was changed for ever. Ancient churches, historic buildings, beautiful streets and cultural treasures were reduced to rubble. Saddest of all was the loss of 1,159 lives, the destruction of 2,500 homes, including the Bishop's House, and the partial wreckage of 46,000 houses.

Such a visitation left an indelible mark on the people. But though bombs and fire destroyed much, they did not destroy the people's spirit, as this cross-section of their reactions clearly reveals.

Two other books have been published on the Bristol blitzes; " Bristol Under Blitz," by Alderman Underdown, Lord Mayor, 1940-41; and " Bristol Bombed," by Mr. F. G. Warne. The first is an official record in words; the second an official record in pictures. Both have great value, but deal with the story from other angles than the one taken in this book. Here you have the story of the rank and file, who tell it in their own way—a story of " blood and tears, and toil and sweat," seasoned with a pinch of our British " saving sense of humour."

As one who passed through all the " Siren Nights," living at the time in one of the unlucky spots, I pay tribute to the magnificent courage of the people, especially the children and those advanced in years. I extend this tribute to the gallant band of auxiliary workers—firemen, fire-watchers, policemen, A.R.P. wardens and their staffs, ambulance units and reception committees without whose help there would have been very little of the city left and the casualties would have been very much greater.

As for the doctors and nurses and hospital staffs—we can never repay our debt to them. I hope that the proceeds from this little book will be of some material help in enabling them to continue their work of mercy in these, more or less, sirenless days.

I am indebted to all who have sent in contributions to this book; without their co-operation it could not have been compiled. My thanks are due, too, to the Bishop of Bristol for his foreword, to Sir Hugh Elles, Regional Commissioner, for giving me access to the records detailed in Part III., to the Editors of the Bristol papers for permission to glean items from their files and for inserting my letters in their columns, to the Publishers for their public spirit in seeing the book through the press in spite of many difficulties, to Mr. H. W. Brand, Assistant Education Officer, for reading the proofs, and especially to Miss Beryl Thornborough, formerly a student of the West of England College of Art, for her fine series of wood engravings and book jacket, and her help in deciding many matters of detail.

S.P.S.

Church of the Ascension,
Mount Hill, Hanham, Bristol.
   November, 1943.

7

Bristol Siren Nights

PART I

DIARIES OF THE BLITZ

Readers of " Pepys's Diary " will agree that it is from his pages that we are enabled to build up the best mental picture of the Fire of London. He tells of the awful magnificence of the scene, of getting his bags of gold into the office ready to carry away, of poor people staying in their houses " as long as till the very fire touched them," and even of the pigeons which were " loth to leave their houses, but hovered about the windows and balconys, till they burned their wings, and fell down."

Bristol has not lacked her diarists during these grim years of war, and from their pages, no doubt, a full and graphic account of the blitzes on our city could be compiled. A number of these diaries has been sent to me in whole or in part, and from them much of what follows in this book has been derived. Owing to lack of space, due to paper restrictions, I have only been able to give selections from a few of them.

But the diary of Mr. W. A. Hares is so " Pepysesque," that it is appearing just as it was received. This well-kept diary, written on the spot, gives the most vivid and accurate account of the bombing of a great city I have come across. It is of more value than many photographs, for it preserves the exact " atmosphere " created among the people who were called upon to endure such ordeals. It reveals, too, the amazing coolness of those who " stuck it."

None of those mentioned in this diary, as far as I know, received any decorations. Perhaps it will be a sufficient reward to them, and hundreds of other nameless heroes, that it occupies a place of honour in this book!

I.—A BROADMEAD DIARY

(By W. A. HARES, 9 Merchant Street, 1)

Extract from Letter: "After a couple of years these episodes seem a trifle melodramatic, but they were written directly after each raid, and there may be in them something of interest to your readers."

THE FIRST BLITZ
Sunday-Monday, November 24th—25th, 1940

My night off, and I take no notice of the early siren, but get ready to go to meet the wife and children in Old Market Street. Heavy gun fire! But I'm used to that, and it gives me no concern, but planes seem to be very low.

Suddenly the sky is lit with several flares. New experience, this. And I begin to get worried. Relieved to find wife and kiddies going into a nearby shelter. People are running like hell! There is a tension in the air like the prelude to a heavy thunderstorm. Little we know what we'll have to face before the night's out. But I get: my family home just as the first bombs start to fall.

The sky is now lit up with different coloured flares; the barrage is terrific, and the air is filled with the constant drone of Jerry planes, the scream of falling bombs and the thunder of their explosion. See my mates. "We're in for a pasting to-night!" Both of them seem to think discretion the better part of valour. Can't blame them, anyway. Got a very queer feeling myself; I'm terribly dry, and I don't quite know what to do, but I decide I'll try and see it through.

Incendiaries start to fall in our own neighbourhood. Several fires in the City; more—and heavier—bombs dropping. Still windy, and the fires spread; new fires springing up now, adding a spectacular effect to the inferno of bombs and gunfire. Beginning to get used to it!

Incendiaries fall across the Barton. Two fall in our street: one on Jones's warehouse starts to smoke and burn. People trying to extinguish them with buckets of water. Terrific barrage: shell cap falls through a window, and I pick it up. Pick up another one that falls just where I am standing. Two early souvenirs!

German planes keep coming over. Don't feel so frightened now. But the centre of the city is one blazing mass, and the Jerries are plastering the fires with all they have. WHAT A NIGHT. Jones's warehouse enveloped in flames; firemen say they can do nothing. Everybody seems very calm, though none seem to know just what to do.

I go to the Warden's Post to see if anything can be done to stop the fires in our street. Little help forthcoming. The two lady telephonists — both perfectly calm — are working like the devil, trying to deal with the chaotic conditions.

More incendiaries, more bombs, more big fires. Hell is released on our city. Many soldiers are doing good work, but we've still no Fire Auxiliaries to deal with the local fires. Frontages now begin to collapse! The din is tremendous. Glass and debris are scattered everywhere. Flames now spread to adjacent buildings. Soldiers shout for shovels to beat out the flames. It seems hopeless now, for the water supply has failed.

Mrs. S. is a heroine. She's making tea for everyone. The landlord of one pub is ready to joke, and tells customers that drinks are on the house, as he does not think there'll be a pub there in the morning! Horses, terror-stricken, are running wild in the streets.

Jones's fire is now dying out. But the Barton Warehouse is a blazing beacon. Jerry's still letting us have it every minute. Think that I'm now accustomed to the bombs and the din, but when a fire-

" Frontages now begin to collapse."

bomb falls on Llewellins & James in the Green, I'm really terrified. I'm caught in the middle of the street. I can't run; I can't duck; I can't shout. It's a ghastly sensation. I just want to gaze and see where the bomb falls. Like an express train with chains rattling, it comes hissing through the air, and falls with a dull thud. Four more come whistling down in Castle Street.

I recover from that shock. Nothing matters any more now, surely! C. and N. have come into the house to die together. "God help us if anything should fall on our factory." They're not showing up too well.

Jones's warehouse is now burnt out, but the adjoining buildings are burning furiously. Soldiers are trying to beat out the flames with coats and caps. It's hopeless. We've no fire-pumps, although there

10

is a river flowing beneath the road, and the hoses could be passed through the many manholes.

More bombs fall on Broadmead. John Hall's starts to blaze. I pick up with a soldier who's got plenty of guts. People start salvaging from the apparently doomed shops and houses. It looks as if the whole block will be gutted. But there's still no sign of any firemen. WHERE THE HELL ARE THEY? Llewellins and James is now ablaze. What a night! And what a party!!

My soldier pal gets a pump from somewhere and we try to put a fire out on the top of Price's roof. We smash in Hobson & Morris's door but cannot get to the fire from inside. Then a fireman lets us have a ladder, and up goes the soldier and I start to pump like hell. Now we get some assistance, although, the buildings across the street are quite beyond control. The café is burning. So is Lenton's, now set alight by the flying sparks carried by the rising wind. J. Hall's now a raging mass. Castle Green is too, and Llewellins & James's seems to be white hot. Bombs and more bombs! Barton Warehouses are nearly burnt out; but the fire is now raging on the other side of the street. A truly majestic sight—oddly enough—from our roof.

Don't seem to mind bombs now. Suppose I have got used to them, or else it's because I've seen other people ignore them. Funny how you can get used to anything if you have to.

Auxiliary pumps are now on the job. It's a crew from outside, and they don't know where the hydrants or manholes are. Eventually they are told of manholes, but have trouble with the covers and it seems hours before they manage to prise them open. Now that the pumps are going and the firemen get busy, it sort of gives you a comforting feeling. Takes your mind off Jerries and bombs!

What a night. Don't think it possible to survive the raid, although the fires that surround us are a sight no-one could ever forget. Jerry seems to be easing off. Planes not coming in so fast, nor does the barrage seem so continuous. No idea of the time. My eyes are one streaming mass, and I can hardly see.

Find the street strewn with cobble stones. Soldier says one just missed him and that he'd better move his car from the blaze. That was the last I saw of him. He was a great lad.

Tell my wife it will probably go on until two a.m. Jerry now seems to have spent his force. He's only coming over occasionally, but what a beacon he has lit aided by the wind! Like a snowstorm; only this " snow " is red and black.

Firemen doing good work and some of the fires are burning themselves out. Blitz seems to have finished. Suppose Jerry's used up all his planes and bombs. Only sounds now are the pumps, the crackling of the flames, and the falling masonry.

GLORY BE! IT'S THE ALL CLEAR. What a marvellous sound, and what a reprieve from hell. I never expected to hear it again, and I really can't believe I'm hearing it now. The first blitz is ended . . . but the fires rage on.

THE SECOND BLITZ

Monday-Tuesday, December 2nd-3rd, 1940

Siren goes. N. and A. have not arrived yet. I'm listening to the News, but the gun-fire is very heavy. Look out and see flares dropping over Clifton way. Tell Mr. C. they've started their nonsense again.

My other two mates have left us in the lurch again. Only two of us to look after three buildings. Have to make wife take shelter. Tell her we're in for another pasting.

Plenty of planes in the sky. Intermittent gun-fire. Seems as if Avonmouth is getting it.

Tell a young lady to take cover. Give same warning to a young man and his girl-friend, who seems very frightened, but who says that she has only to die once. Pick up with a deaf fellow, and ask him to lend me a hand. He's quite willing, and shows no fear. He's been to sea and has been torpedoed. Just the right man in a pinch!

Bombs dropping nearer now. Have to lay down several times. Somehow, though, it's not like the first night. I suppose the thought of getting through one blitz makes it an odds-on chance of seeing this lot over. Big blaze in middle of town, and Jerries seem to be concentrating on that.

Messrs. C. and B. give me a look up. The first blitz has given us the comradeship of old campaigners, and we all seek to give what help we can to each other.

Bombs whistling down. Funny to see the deaf man fall down when I do, like a one-man act. There's a very close one!! We're covered with blue sparks. Everything seems to rock.

The wife's all right, although she cannot get the children to sleep. The people in the house are now quite all right. The wife shows them how to keep their chins up.

Fires are now blazing in the Croft, North Street and the middle of the town. Someone tells me that the station has copped it and that most of the early stuff fell Westbury way.

Barrage intermittent. Not so continuous as the first blitz. Policeman says our planes are up. Then we get some excitement in our sector. Incendiaries fall across the Friar's Roof, and the beams start to blaze. I go and tell them what has happened and as there is another lot burning round the garage petrol pumps, I cycle round to the Wardens' Post to report it.

Return to find Mr. T., the caretaker, and a policeman, silhouetted against the red glow of a big fire across Newfoundland Street, taking no notice of the stuff that is falling. Policeman shouts to Mr. T. to pump harder. Then, with a swish, another string of fire bombs comes sailing down across the road. We think they have missed us, and go across the road to see where they have fallen.

Glory be! Our own building's ablaze. I didn't know what to think for the moment. The fire seemed to be out of control in a few minutes. I shouted to " Deaffy " to follow me, and we rush up the stairs. Fire has caught the beams and there is the sound of hissing.

12

"Deaffy" starts to put out the flames on the second floor with his foot and cap. I rush to the top floor and let the bomb there have it with a bucketful of water. The worst thing I could have done, for the whole thing went up in a sheet of white flame. Fire seemed to spread all around me. I got panicky, and started to back away. Fell over a bucket of sand. Threw sand on to the fire, and was surprised to see the flames die down.

"Deaffy" had now stamped and almost put out the fire on the second floor; we got to work with stirrup pump, and in no time it seemed that the job was finished. So I stuck out my chest.

The fires to-night seem to have been got under control much quicker than I thought they would. Practice must make perfect. Harris's, across the road, starts to burn. Flames coming from glass fanlight. Looks like a big fire. Dash round to the Warden's Post, but a messenger is already on the way. On returning, a Jerry plane comes in low and lets go his load of hate. It falls quite near, and my bike seems to be sucked across the road. Another explosion. Phew! That was a close 'un.

Auxiliaries on the job pretty quickly. Not long before water is being pumped on to the flames. But another building is doomed. Another big fire for Jerry to play on.

Again we are between two fires, because the Dockland Settlement and buildings beyond are blazing. But despite to-night's fires, there is not the same excitement as there was on the first night's blitz. Must be getting *blasé*.

Things are now easing off and we now wait for the All Clear. Jerry has not had it all his own way to-night, and I don't think he has done so much damage—considering the length of the raid—as he did the first time.

THE THIRD BLITZ

Friday-Saturday, December 6th-7th, 1940

Warning. All on duty, be ready for anything. Look forward to some action. Gun-fire heavy. Plenty of planes about. Some flares dropped but it seems the Jerries are after something else to-night.

Then fire-watcher calls out to us to observe a plane in the search-lights. Planes are very low to-night. Some damned good pilots, I should think. Flares over Temple Meads. We are all waiting for something to happen.

More planes, swarms of them, although they all seem to be passing over the town, and leaving us alone. Everyone appears to be on tip-toe to-night. Now a Jerry plane makes a smoke sign. Think at first it has been hit by the Ack-Ack, but it passes out of sight.

More flares. Still no action. Then we get a thrill. Two planes come in, one with smoke pouring from its tail; the other behind it with navigation lights full on. They pass over, and the first plane

13

makes a complete circle of white smoke. Tell the wife to expect it—hot and heavy.

A few incendiaries fall. One near the "Mail Coach," and a War Reserve Constable takes a flying kick at it. It's soon put out. Then comes the heavy stuff. There is a glow in the sky from the docks, and over Temple Meads and Redcliffe way fires start to burn furiously. We wait for more incendiaries, though there seems little doing in our particular neighbourhood.

City Mill catches fire, but firemen are soon on the job. It's blazing fiercely. Firemen told of manholes in the street, and they get to work quickly, and soon have the pumps going. Jerry is still coming over, but there seems to be several minute intervals between the planes.

Wife gets firemen some tea, but they are too busy to drink it. A big and heavy direct hit on the little "Gem" Cinema is scored. Luckily the fire-watcher had moved away in time. Mr. B. says it lifted him off the floor.

To-night it seems that most of the fires are quickly got under control, and everybody carried on just as a matter of fact. If a big-'un falls near, they joke about it, and people are out in the streets watching the fire-fighters.

City Mill now well under control, but there's a big fire in Bridge Street.

Early All Clear. Another blitz has been borne and survived!

THE FOURTH BLITZ

Friday-Saturday, January 3rd-4th, 1941

Planes over. One comes in very low; it's a single-engined plane and we think it's one of our own night-fighters until the guns open up. What a lovely tone Percy's got! Gives all of us plenty of confidence!

S. has not arrived. Wonder where he's got to. There is a very heavy barrage and planes are coming in low, and swiftly. Flares drop over Easton way. More over City centre. Warn people in street to expect something pretty soon, and tell them to get water and pumps ready.

Incendiaries drop in Weir, and J. chases off against my orders and flings a bucket of water over one. Up she goes in a sheet of flame. J.'s clothes are burnt and he hurts his side.

S. turns up with "sails in the wind," and says he has been putting out fire bombs. I curse him a bit, but he has had too many and it is useless to tell him anything. Put a man on with Mr. C., but he funks it and makes off to a shelter.

Street fire-watchers are chasing about and doing good work all over the place. Then down across the street and buildings falls another string of incendiaries. Several are on the Friars, more around the garage. Plenty are burning in the street and one is burning on the Coroner's Court.

14

Our buildings are apparently all right. So I smash in the C.C. windows and then realise it's a very high roof and has got to be tackled from outside. No ladder about, so I have to climb the drainpipe. Get a shovel, tie it on to my walking stick, then shin up the drainpipe, and clamber on to the roof.

By now Mr. T. and Les are out and getting the water ready. The incendiary is fizzing away merrily, and I start shovelling it over the tiles bit by bit. It's a very poor bomb with hardly any kick in it, although if left it could have caused another fire.

Les hands me up a bucket of water and I succeed in putting out the burning woodwork. Getting off the roof is a darn sight more difficult, and the water has now frozen and the tiles are one sheet of ice. Keep thinking of the iron spiked railings in case I should slip! Very nasty work.

Big fires across the river. Appears that the docks are the main object to-night. Jones's in Broadmead is burning but the firemen are soon there, and I think it will soon be out. The water is freezing, as it leaks from the hoses. Very difficult to get about.

The All Clear goes. . . .

"Very nasty work."

A second warning. Now for the heavy stuff, think I, and I'm not far wrong. It seems that Jerry has altered his tactics, for now single-engined machines come in very low; drop one H.E. and then scoot like the devil away from the barrage. Some very good target bombing to-night and he's not wasting many. Although we are on the edge of the target area and the big ones are whining down quite regularly, you have a feeling that your own district will not get it.

The factory is shaken several times, and there is a great mushroom of smoke and debris from a large bomb that lands in the ruins at the top of Bridge Street. Barrage seems to make everything vibrate and we wonder when it is going to end. The docks and Redcliffe Street are one blazing mass, providing Jerry with a wonderful target, and doesn't he play on it! Hour after hour it goes on, although the planes are now not so persistent. The monotony of it makes me tired. Some of the watchers pack up and go home. You feel there will be no more incendiaries to deal with and I get in the chair and have forty winks. The place is rocked by a very near one. So it goes on. The All Clear goes and so ends our first all-night blitz.

15

SHORT RAID ON EASTVILLE AND EAST BRISTOL

Wednesday-Thursday, February 26th-27th, 1941

Planes over. Heavy gunfire. Am relating a few past experiences to the new voluntary watchers, when a plane comes in very low and lets go several bombs. We all fall flat and expect a lot more, but nothing happens.

There's a huge glow in the sky from Eastville way and one of the watchers tells of a huge momentary flash. Incendiaries are falling away to the east of us mixed with a few H.E.s.

Fire-watchers are discussing the whereabouts of the fires when all at once the familiar hiss of a shower of incendiaries sends us all scuttling for cover. I am standing in the doorway with F.K. The other two men are in the boiler house having supper. As I dive through the door I notice some fire bombs in the Friars, one in Evans' and the street littered with them—a pretty sight! Looks as if the whole neighbourhood is on fire.

Top floor is ablaze. My pals tear up over the stairs with me. What a sight meets our gaze! There is fire dripping through from the office into the carton room, and all the boxes are blazing. Up the stairs again there is molten magnesium flowing from the top floor setting the lift shaft alight. The incendiary in the office is certainly going some, and I can see in S.'s room there is another making a hell of a mess. It's a fire-fighter's bad dream—you don't know which to start on first.

My three mates are on the top floor giving another the works. So I tackle the one in the office. No time for "finessing" with stirrup pump or other fancy tackle. Two buckets of water straight on the damn thing, and up she goes. *Then some sand on top.* I rush down to the boxroom on the next floor. Another couple of buckets of water dampens down the blazing cartons, and J. throws some more over the now burning woodwork.

Up into the form room where another incendiary is lodged in the rafters. We throw water, but cannot reach it. We throw sand over the burning papers, drench the bench with water. Leave that and dash back to the office where the first one is getting a hold on the tables and stock. C. goes up to the bomb, thinking it is a blazing gaspipe, as it is lodged on the wall horizontally. Approaches the bomb with a bucket of water, and attempts to pour the water on to the fire. The bomb blazes more furiously; C. jumps! And throws the bucket as well. It makes me laugh.

Things are getting pretty sticky with fires going in five different places, so J. puts a call through for the Fire Brigade. We keep pegging away at the fires, first one then the other, and gradually get all of them under control. It's the hottest thirty minutes I have ever experienced, and by the time the Brigade arrived they were only needed to extinguish a fire in the Mail Coach.

16

I then look out, and think that I shall see the whole neighbourhood on fire. But all the fires are well under control now, and have been "outed" successfully. It was some damn good practice for all of us, and I feel proud the way my crew dealt with the situation. There is no doubt that if any one of us had funked it the whole building would have gone up, as we had no assistance from outside.

Planes were still over, but it seemed that the raid had fizzled out and an early All Clear gave us a chance of looking back on a job well done.

THE FIFTH BLITZ

Sunday-Monday, March 16th-17th, 1941

Planes over. Heavy gunfire. Flares, incendiaries, and bombs begin falling almost immediately. Big fire started at Lawrence Hill. Planes are coming in continuously. Seems that we're in for another picnic. Wonder what the night will bring forth.

The Huns are certainly mixing them well to-night. Not much chance of their missing the town with the fires they have started so early. Nothing happening just around us, so we go to the top floor to see what and where things are occurring. Two or three fires burning to the east and smoke and flame begins to pour from a factory in the Croft. The blue incandescent light of exploding incendiaries can be seen in several different directions, and bunches of chandelier flares are being continually dropped.

Ground defences are firing tracer shells. Barrage over-head provides suitable "incidental music," interrupted by the scream of high explosives. We get tired of ducking and just anticipate where they are likely to fall. I watch a string of incendiaries bursting as they strike the roofs of Ellbroad Street. They seem to be coming straight for the factory, and then take a sudden turn across the ruins of Castle Street, where they are quite harmless. Another lot falls straight up Philadelphia Street—explosive incendiaries, this time—and these are followed by a stick of H.E.'s which pass right over the buildings and fall with tremendous explosions in City and Ashley Roads.

Anderson's and the buildings around are now a huge burning mass, but still the Hun has not had enough. A plane comes in very low and right over Kingsdown and Stokes Croft, lets go both heavy explosive and incendiaries. It seemed that the blast of the bombs temporarily smothered the fire.

Planes are easing off now. Gunfire only spasmodic. A lull ensues, and the All Clear sounds.

Another siren wail. Surely Jerry has had enough for one night! But no. The fires he previously started guide him, but this time the bombs seem to be aimed at residential areas. It goes on hour after hour, until you are sickened utterly by the futility and continued hopelessness of it all. You no longer pay any heed when a stick of bombs falls quite near. In fact, I was surprised to see the explosion

17

of a big 'un before the whistle of it had ceased. Though I've been through several blitzes and bombs have fallen all round, this is the first time I have actually seen the eruption of flame and debris. It left me with a very queer and helpless feeling. The All Clear sounded, and another memorable night has been safely passed through.

THE SIXTH BLITZ.

Friday-Saturday, April 11th-12th, 1941

Good Friday. It's very quiet this evening, and we're really not expecting anything to happen. The siren goes and we stand by as usual.

In come the planes. The barrage opens up immediately, but unlike the first blitzes, there are now plenty of firewatchers. Matters are more organised; the novelty of being subjected to aerial bombardment has faded, and we know our own capabilities to deal with any fire bombs that fall in the district.

Unable to see much in the street we go up to the top floor to take a look if anything should happen. It's not a bad view; orange and red flares drift slowly down, the red bursts of the ack-ack shells followed by the drifting white haloes light the sky whilst we wait for the more vigorous and devastating part of the play to begin.

With a terrific shriek a large bomb falls on Broadmead—a very early present! Then a string of incendiaries swishes across Cotham and beyond. We watch a series of different lines of incendiaries and applaud or criticise when they are not outed quickly or allowed to take hold. In quick succession five lots are plotted and it is now apparent that Jerry needs more than incendiaries to get the people of this town panicky. In spite of this, there are big fires raging in Cheltenham Road, Stokes Croft and Kingsdown, and it seems that Jerry is determined to increase these.

My mates and I stand looking out of the windows wondering if and when anything is coming our way. It seems again we are on the edge of things and have got to be content with the role of spectators. Then, in the distance, the blue incandescent light of exploding fire bombs is seen down across the roofs and streets starting from the top of the Croft, coming half-way down then taking a S.W. turn towards us. We watch them come nearer—Brunswick Square, Rosemary Street and up the Friars. I shout to my mates to duck under the table, expecting to have the rest right through our own roof.

Seconds pass. We think it's all right now, and one of us suggests we go and look for souvenirs. Coming down the stairs we get a shock. There is our souvenir burning away in the office. Using the now successful method of past raids, I let the bomb have a full bucket of water. Up she goes in a sheet of flame and sparks. Harry comes behind with the sandbags and dumps them on top, and Bert brings up the rear with two more buckets of water. Beyond a little mess no damage is done.

18

We now go down to the street to see if any more had dropped near. What a difference from the first blitzes when a single fire bomb could do tremendous damage through the lack of training and knowledge! The All Clear goes, and we prepare for a night's rest.

But we have no luck. Off goes Moaning Minnie again, and we get ready for the second half of the show.

The barrage, which had tailed off considerably during the last hour now opens up again with fresh intensity, and whilst watching the innumerable bursts in the sky we get the surprise of our lives. The great black shapes of a COUPLE OF GERMAN BOMBERS come sailing in well below the balloons. With three guns firing from them at the balloons and the ground defences they pass right overhead, and let their load of hate fall near the Centre.

"I let the bomb have a full bucket of water."

The attack now shifts to the middle of the city, and fires spring up in Redcliffe Street, the Centre, and Park Street. They quickly get out of hand, and become beacons—a guide for far more terrific bombing. A few more incendiaries across Stokes Croft, St. Michael's Hill, and Park Row. Big fire starts near gasometer at the back of the Eye Hospital.

Hell let loose again; terrific bomb attack. Fire in Park Street now assumes huge proportions, and flames leap high into the air, reminiscent of the first blitz.

Raid goes on till early morning, by which time the early fires had died down, and I think everybody had had just about enough.

2.—FROM A HEADMASTER'S DIARY

(This is an extract from the diary of Mr. M. E. Brodie, Headmaster of Stokes Croft Endowed School. Both his school and his home were totally destroyed in the first blitz, and he was blasted out of two houses subsequently.—Ed.).

My wife, son and I lived on the premises of the 220 years old school at the bottom of Stokes Croft, to which was attached the almshouses, occupied in 1940 by four women and one man. Their ages ranged from 60 to 90.

We had just finished our tea on November 24th, 1940, when the sirens sounded. I was in Home Guard uniform, and our son, employed in the Post Office Engineering Department, was in his working clothes.

One of the first flares drifted slowly down, illuminating our courtyard and buildings, and the shops in Stokes Croft. As an old Bomber Pilot I knew that this was the prelude to a serious attack, so we decided to get the old people from the almshouses into the school basement.

Screams from Stokes Croft warned us of the first shower of incendiary shells which fell between City Road and North Street, and along Jamaica Street as far as King Square. Cridland and Rose's boot factory seemed to be the first building to get well alight, closely followed by the printing works in King Square, and Hornby's in Stokes Croft.

Very soon showers of sparks were blowing across our premises, and we decided to try to get the old people to a safer refuge. We realised, too, that the flames would serve as a target for following bombers. It was impossible to go up or down Stokes Croft, so we led the old folk from the back of the School to the North Street School playground where there was a surface shelter. We had to brush the sparks from our clothes as we went.

It was providential that we moved when we did, for we had only just got away when a high explosive bomb wrecked almshouse and school.

A few minutes previously one old lady had asked me to see that her door was closed, which I did. We had to smother an incendiary which had fallen near her room, so I took this opportunity of fastening her door.

Another old lady had told me that she thought she would be as safe in her room as anywhere else, because she had a cupboard in the corner. It was in her room that the bomb actually exploded, so I think she was glad afterwards that we had hurried her out. I'm glad to say that none were injured, although the explosion of the bomb made the shelter rock. This is not surprising for the shelter was barely twenty yards from the back of the school.

At one time we seemed to be ringed with fires and the sparks from the flames, and more than once wondered if we should live to see the morning. It was difficult, at times, to tell the difference between a bursting bomb and the collapse of a building.

SOME REFLECTIONS ON THE ABOVE

As in battle, I have noticed that the real heroes are the people who carry on and stand their ground in spite of dangers.

Three people stand out in my memory in this respect.

One was a fireman in Stokes Croft who, at the height of the raid, nodded towards the mounting flames and complained: " No water!" I left him standing there, waiting until water should be available and he and his comrades could tackle their colossal task. Their pump was wrecked by a H.E. a few minutes later, and several of its crew were killed.

Another was a lady warden at the post in Brunswick Square. She looked hot, tired, and dirty, and was staring helplessly at a burning timber yard. She had come through the city during the raid in order to report for duty. Quietly and efficiently she directed our efforts to find shelter for the old people.

The third was the lady in charge of the Church Army Shelter in Brunswick Square. Calmly and patiently she was leading the people to the warmth and shelter inside. Her quiet, kindly manner was like a tonic to the homeless people whom she mothered.

It will be noticed that each of these three was doing his/her duty, not by rushing too and fro and getting excited, but by moving about quietly and attending to the task in hand in spite of imminent danger.

One curious thing I noticed after the school was hit. The school telephone, candlestick pattern, used to stand in the hall at the front of the school. I discovered it standing in the far corner of the playground upright, and the receiver still hanging on its hook!

TAIL-PIECE

It was rather amusing the following morning to hear, while making my way through people gathered in Stokes Croft, that the schoolmaster had been killed, his wife seriously injured and in the B.R.I., that their son was missing, and that rescue squads were digging for the bodies of the old people!

3.—ON CHRISTMAS STEPS

(MISS M. FAGNANI, 52, Colston Street.)

BLITZ of 24/11/40

Jerry is here early to-night. Siren went five minutes ago. Yes, he's here all right. Some bombs are being dropped and a fire has started already to the east of us. I've got a nasty feeling in my tummy too at this moment. God grant it is going to be all right for us. 11.5 p.m. same night: We've been through hell. Never have I experienced anything like it. Tummy still wobbly. Fires and bombs everywhere. Went to the cellar at first, but couldn't settle down, so went to the sitting-room. We didn't need any light for the room was lit up with the glare of the fires. Wine Street looks as if it is no more. Fires all seem centred in that direction, though up the hill at the back of our place there are fires also. One looks like the Prince's Theatre. Our sitting-room window woodwork is so hot you can hardly bear your hand on it. The house rocks as the bombs drop. It is like a " Wellsonian Drama " come true. I must pay my tribute to the firemen. All the time the dreadful bombing was at its height one of them swayed about on a water tower playing on the fire at Budgett's wholesale warehouse. Sometimes he was completely obliterated by the great clouds of smoke, but always when it cleared he was still there, though Jerry kept bombing time after time. If ever a chap deserved the George Cross he did.

Next Morning: Well, it was over at last, and we got through but only by a miracle, like hundreds more. From our top storey at 9 a.m. the next morning the city looked bruised and battered. Its heart was plucked out, almost. Our back yard is littered with grey ashes and burnt bits of paper. The streets are grey and the people seem stunned. But we shall get over it. Jerry is not going to get away with it, never fear. Our turn will come   .   .   .!

BLITZ of 4/12/40

We have had our second blitz, nearer to us this time. A bomb exploded a hundred yards away, but we only caught the blast up here. Our only trouble was broken windows in house and shop, but such details are small compared with others. My greatest anxiety came from my old step-father who is 77. He *would* go up from the cellar to investigate. When he came down he said that so far we were intact, but he had some pieces of tile and red earth in his hands, and said the street was strewn with it. We found the next morning that the tiles and red earth had come from the churchyard of St. Michael's, our parish church on the hill. A huge bomb had fallen just outside the crypt in which hundreds of people were sheltering. None of them was hurt! Small portions of old tombstones and old bones from the graves were hurled into the top rooms of houses nearby. I'm a bit edgy, but mustn't show the white feather, and above all I must keep my faith in God whatever happens.

22

BLITZ of 3/1/41

Bristol was blitzed again last night. For twelve solid hours my neighbour and I sat in our cellar. My step-father was up and down all the time keeping watch. We had the two cats with us, and my Scottie. He's been a brick through all the raids. He lays at my feet all the time and only moved when the actual bombs fall. He seems to be able to sense them coming, because his ears go up and then you hear that dreadful swishing and screaming as they reach the earth. That sound gets me really more than the actual crashing. It was cold in the cellar where we were huddled together, so during one of the " stills " I went upstairs and made some Oxo. At that moment bang went a bomb—and the Oxo! I went hastily to earth again, where we stopped until the finish.

It was a cruel and fiendish attack. Hospitals, churches and houses were all hit—no military objectives at all. The almshouses at the top of the Steps had incendiaries, but they were put out promptly by firewatchers. We heard of many tragedies, too numerous to remember. But we came out all right once more, which every time I call a miracle, because we are right in the midst of it all.

BLITZ of 16/3/41

This has been the worst blitz so far, and that's saying a lot. Incendiaries were everywhere; some fell on the roof of St. Michael's and some two doors away from us, gutting the place. Wardens came through our place and over our roof to tackle them. They were like a regiment of soldiers marching up and down the stairs. My old step-father was in his element up in the attic, handing out the water, and then directing them how to climb the tiles. But he gave me one panicky moment. I came up from the cellar to see how things were getting on, when I heard heavy footsteps coming down the attic stairs, and much heaving and groaning, as I thought. Then I heard a voice saying, " Have you got hold all right?" etc., etc. And I thought, " Oh, my God, that's Pa; it's finished him!" I waited in fear and trepidation for them to get down with their burden. When they did I found they were carrying between them a huge bag of sand weighing at least a cwt. They had lugged it all the way up, and had to lug it back again! I told them I thought they were bringing Pa down. They laughed and said: " He's all right; he's a great help to us up there. You needn't worry over him!"

(Well done, Pa! And he suffers from chronic asthma!—Ed.)

GOOD FRIDAY BLITZ. 11/4/41

The most terrifying experience of all. Jerry came over and bombed us again here in the Centre. After enduring that horror for two hours the All Clear went, but fifteen minutes afterwards the Alert sounded again, and we had it even worse. It was indescribable, but the people were wonderful. Our poor city was unmercifully scarred once more. To make it worse for us our neighbour on our left dropped dead. He was found so by the wardens; his invalid wife was lying beside him. She had managed to crawl out of her couch bed and had been calling for help for two hours. We heard a peculiar cry while in the cellar amidst the noise of the hell outside, but we thought it was a cat somewhere. Little did we dream of the tragedy that had taken place next door.

Our sitting-rooms is crowded with cases and belongings of most people from the " Steps " who have evacuated owing to a time-bomb being in the fried-fish shop at the bottom. Others are in the church crypt and others with friends. A spot of humour: A couple of old ladies from the almshouse at the top of the " Steps " examining the usual Time-Bomb notice which the' authorities always put up. Out of one of the evacuated shops came a lady, escorted by a policeman, carrying a wireless unit which a customer particularly wanted. As she passed by the old ladies one of them exclaimed, " Good gracious! Is *that* the bomb?"

FOLLOWING MONDAY

It is a strange and awful Eastertide for Bristol, and the city is full of morbid sightseers, whom I have no time for. All the big papers on Sunday have given us a good write up; they say we have had the worst raid outside of London so far, and Bristol is the worst blitzed city of the lot. So if we exist at the end of the war we shall have something to feel proud about for having " stayed put." Though I am no church-goer, I believe in God, and through it all I have never lost my faith.

4.—THREE SAVED BY A WHISTLE

(LADY WARDEN. Post C1, B Div., Bedminster.)

" *The shelter was reached.*"

Good Friday night, 1941! The sirens had gone twice. The first time nothing happened, and so the All Clear went early. But about twenty minutes later they went again, and things began to happen. A Lady Warden was going the rounds of the shelters just to cheer up the people, when suddenly " the heavens opened up." The Warden pops into a nearby shelter, and when it gets quiet slips along to the next. This holds 200 people and it is packed. It is situated in front of a " cabinet works," but it is underground and an excellent shelter. Incendiaries start falling, and H.E.'s too. The works catch fire and a man gets " windy " and upsets the others.

They all make a wild dash to get out. Little children were in danger of being trampled on, and something must be done.

The street shelters were already full, so the Warden suggests taking a few people up to her own private shelter—an Anderson in her garden. Picking up a little girl, about 4, and followed by the child's mother, and her brother, a lad of 15, the four set out. It was only about 150 yards, but H.E.'s were dropping and the planes overhead were so low that at times they could be seen, so that those 150 yards seemed more like miles. At last the shelter was reached, and no sooner had the door been shut than down came a H.E. just five yards away. The shelter fell in; all were buried with concrete and earth. But the Warden's head and shoulders and arms were free, though her nose was severely cut.

When the Warden had collected her senses, she realised that something must be done to save the other three as well as herself. So she started to blow her whistle. The neighbours at first thought it was the signal for more incendiaries, but the Warden kept on blowing and then help came from two men neighbours. Though the Warden was badly knocked about she was able to tell the rescuers that there were three others in difficulties beside herself. So after getting more help the "digging out" began. The little girl first—alive, but with leg injuries; then the mother—also alive, but with leg injuries; then the Warden with leg injuries and concussion. Finally the boy—who was dead. But for that whistle all four would have died. The Warden was home eight months, and then returned to duty and is still carrying on with her job, and the little girl and her mother are both fit again.

(The writer of the above was the lady Warden.—Ed.).

5.—FROM A LITTLE PATIENT

(MRS. A. E. TAYLOR, 16, Avon View, Keynsham.)

(Though this letter was written from the children's Orthopædic Hospital, Coombe Park, Bath, we feel that it ought to be included in this book as it is typical of the splendid spirit shown even by the small inmates of our hospitals during a blitz. This little girl wrote this letter to her parents the day after the first heavy raid on Bath. She was ten years old at the time, and was suffering from a tubercular foot. As her mother said in a covering letter: "It is a simple, unvarnished account of the raid as seen through the eyes of a sick child in hospital, and as such it has an interest. I have heard since, from the sister of the ward, that the behaviour of the young nurses—little more than children themselves—was splendid."—Ed.).

Here is the letter, just as it was written: —

" Dear Mamma and Daddy,

" Did you have a raid last night and was it very bad? We had three Alerts, the first a few guns, and all the day nurses appeared in all sorts of clothes, then the All Clear sounded and we went to sleep.

" Next came another warning and All Clear without any guns or noise. Then, an Alert with a lot of noise and anti-aircraft guns, machine-guns and bombs. Of course the day nurses got up again, and when we heard a bomb or two they lifted us out, bedclothes and all and popped us under the beds. Then the black-out blind would keep going up, and then a soldier in blue and a nurse and a man with a white night-shirt and night-cap came and put chairs on top of it. When it went up we saw a red glow all about and some people started to cry.

"When that stopped there was a low aeroplane and a whistle and a bang, then again much nearer. Then we started potting at him again. Soon after he went away, and we found it was morning with a small hole in the roof the other end of the ward, and a few pieces of broken wood.

"It was funny after to see a short fat nurse and a big tall soldier making a bed together. I hope you did not get it too badly. One of the soldiers has put a new string on my Yo Yo and it works nicely now.

"With lots of love from

PHYLLIDA.

"P.S.—We heard on the wireless in the morning that three enemy planes were shot down. I am enclosing a very baby rainbow that I made. I am now playing my pipe."

6.—THE LAUGH WAS AGAINST HIM

(MR. N. H. LANGRAN, 7, South Grove, Kellaway Avenue.)

It was in the late summer of 1940 when night after night the sirens were giving their warning, usually about 10 o'clock. It was about 1.30 a.m. on this particular morning and the "Red" had been on for some hours. I had just finished my refreshment period at the Police Station mess room and was starting on my patrol which took me to Durdham Downs. A German bomber was over the city, and I could hear the uneven drone of its engines behind me. The searchlights had located it, and it looked like a small silver cross in the sky. The A.A. guns were firing but the bursts appeared to be wide of the mark. In those days, before the blitzes, these single raiders had come so often, flying round the city without dropping bombs, that people had got used to them, and very few bothered to treat them seriously.

Suddenly I heard the whistle of a bomb that seemed to be dropping straight on me—it was my first experience of a bomb. It passed over and I heard the explosion a second or two after. I rose from my flattened position, and learnt from the police pillar that a house had been hit at Westbury-on-Trym; I was to proceed there.

When I arrived some helpers were already there, and I went into the hall. By the light of my torch I saw a man suffering from an injured leg. A civilian was bending over him, dressing the wound, and I was horrified to see that the bandage being used was soiled. I spoke indignantly to the civilian: "Please take that soiled bandage off; I have a clean emergency dressing which I will put on. The leg will have to be washed, too, so wait till I get some water. You don't know, apparently, the elementary rules of first aid." The civilian ignored my advice and continued his work.

I went back to the house, and as the water supply had been put out of action by the bomb, I obtained some from a cistern. A few minutes later I returned to the hall and found that the injured man and his helper had gone. They had both left in an ambulance. Observing that it was a crime that "enthusiastic but ignorant persons should dabble in first aid," I stalked out, but not before I heard the quiet reply: "Yes, the gentleman who did the bandaging, to whom you spoke, was Dr. ——," naming an eminent surgeon of Bristol!

I have often wondered if he was amused or annoyed at my ill-timed comments on his ability. Perhaps he may see this in print and accept my belated apologies.

(Mr. Langran was a War Reserve Policeman serving in the Bristol Constabulary, and was on duty in the city and at Avonmouth during the raids.—Ed.).

7.—FROM A BEDMINSTER WARDEN

(MR. RICH, "Sunnyside," Chestnut Road, Long Ashton.)

It was on the night of the first big raid—Sunday, November 24, 1940. I was making my way to my post (Warden's Post C1, Bedminster) when a stick of bombs fell unpleasantly close to me. But I was unhurt, and ran along the road to the incident. I had travelled about twenty yards when I came a real cropper. Telephone wires were down, and they wrapped themselves about my legs and body like an angry octopus. They twanged most distressingly against my steel helmet, and as I thought they were electric wires I worked myself into a fair panic. At last I freed myself and hurried, much shaken, into a house which had suffered badly.

The scene was pretty grim. A man and his son were both fatally injured. And here was I, a warden whose duty it was to inspire and instil confidence, in a badly shaken state! And then a young girl, a member of the family, suddenly appeared and said in a voice so steady that I shall always remember it: "Will you turn off the gas at the main, warden?" That calm voice steadied me.

It was then I became aware of the smell. It was sickly, sweet and bitter all at the same time. Quite different from anything I had ever smelt before. Looking back it was like a pickle factory and a hospital rolled into one. Of course the thought immediately came to my mind: "Poison gas!" My respirator was out of my bag in a second, and I was just on the point of telling the people in the house to get their masks on when a man dashed in and explained the whole mystery. "Can you smell anything?" I asked. "Of course I can," he replied. "That's all that's left of my chemist's shop—the smell!"

I hurried to the post to report. The telephonist picked up the receiver and looked suddenly alarmed. I knew what the trouble was at once. Those wires! The 'phone was out of action. Bombs were dropping all over the district by now, and yet the messenger-boy never hesitated to set off to the report centre. Perhaps he went a little white in the face, but never questioned his orders. Grand youngsters those boys! They deserve a chapter to themselves. The report centre was at least a mile from the post, and during his perilous journey he had two spills. He was never sure whether the blast blew him off, or whether he tried to duck for dear life—and dear life it was, for many were injured that night.

When he entered the report centre they were just receiving our message over the 'phone. The Post Office had got the line through somehow. Good organisation, this! The strangest part of that episode comes now. Jack, the messenger-boy, was unscathed that night. Yet the next morning the group warden sent Jack on a message, and he skidded on a wet road and injured his shoulder!

8.—A WARDEN'S WIFE

(MRS. M. COLEMAN, 88, Coldharbour Road, 6.)

I was frying some bacon, in fact, had just put a slice in the pan, when the sirens went. A queer feeling ran through my body and seemed to land in my stomach, then luckily disappeared. My husband was sitting waiting for his tea, already in uniform, as the sirens had gone off for several nights round about this time. I was getting acclimatised!

" I got them under the stairs."

The slice of bacon still in the pan, just beginning to sizzle. I turned the light out; we would sup later—perhaps! The barrage took on a more vicious note—a whip-like crack that was familiar. My husband grabbed his tin hat and respirator, and said: "That sounds like us."

I wished him "Cheerio," and started to get our hide-out ready. We had a camp bed under the stairs. I got pillows, blankets and woollen coats for my two baby children (aged 2½ and nine months), who I left in their beds until things seemed dangerous. By now there was a terrific amount of gunfire, so I filled a hot-water bottle, and took a bottle of milk, two mugs and a tin of biscuits to our hide-out; also some cigarettes in case I found a spare moment for one.

I was joined by an elderly lady from the flat above. She said: "It's one of our nights to-night." "Yes," I replied, and at that moment there was a terrific bump nearby. I ran into the nursery and caught up a child in each arm, my heart beating about 200 to the minute. I got them under the stairs with the help of the old lady, put on their coats, and packed them between the blankets. I was in trousers and an overcoat, and we settled ourselves down.

Very heavy thuds shook us every ten minutes or so, and we could hear the planes diving and the bombs whistling overhead, as it seemed. I suppose I was fortunate to have two children who did not wake to the sound of the sirens, gunfire, or even the bombs. The drone of a plane coming slowly nearer and nearer—a dive—a long screaming whistle. "Ye gods," thought I, "this is ours!" The old lady and I automatically grabbed a pillow each and covered the kids, who must come first. A sickening thud! But we're still here. What a miracle! "That was a close one, mummy," said my eldest little chap. "Yes, it was," says I, thinking really, "Thank the Lord you don't realise how near to death you've been."

We now had intervals of about ten minutes in which I managed to give the kids a drink of milk and a biscuit. I was very glad to hear my husband come in about 8.30 to see if we were O.K. He managed to spare time to make a cup of tea for me and my partner under the stairs, and to bring us a few of the kids' toys, pencils and paper. Up to now we had amused them by making shadows on the walls with our fingers, and lots of other simple little things. They seem simple now—but they didn't then!

I wished my husband another "Cheerio," and we settled down again. I was nearly dozing when I heard a kind of shout or yell. Something gripped my throat. "My husband!" I thought. "Something's hit him. He has fallen. Oh, dear Lord, keep him safe!" I had a tiny feeling that he was all right, but also a strong feeling that he might be hurt. I wanted to run out and see, but the old lady was half-dazed, and both kids were tucked tight by me. That awful whistling again and another sickening thud! But I stayed put.

I sat back and thought of what his little family would do without him. Lots of wives lost their husbands these days; we were all in this fight—even the kids! They ran as great a risk here under the stairs as the wardens and ambulance-drivers; no one knew where or what the bombs would hit after whistling down. All the same, thinking of trying to manage without my husband brought a few tears which I could not hide from my eldest boy. "Are you worried about something?" he asked. "No, dear," I replied, "only tired," and we ducked quickly under the pillows again.

By now my little one was getting sleepy, so I settled him down, nice and cosy. I thought he was nearly asleep, when suddenly he got up again and exclaimed: "Dada!" How I thanked my lucky stars! In he walked to see if we were still O.K. He told me a little of what had happened—a school near-by had been badly hit but no one hurt. I thought by now that our house must be the only one

29

standing in the road, and was very surprised to hear that nothing had come nearer than 100 yards!

It went on till midnight, by which time my kids had both dropped off after a lot of persuasion, and I was able to stretch my legs a little. What a relief!

But a greater relief was soon to follow, the All Clear rang out, as if to say: "Don't worry; it's all over now!" What a wonderful sound it is! And yet for the poor folk who were now wounded or had lost dear ones, it was a terrible sound. Every time they hear it they can see themselves standing by ruins, just saying: "I've lost him, or her, or them."

I kept thinking to myself for a long time when it was all over how lucky I had been. I went outside and saw the fires. They looked wicked, somehow. People were bustling home who had been held up in shelters. A curious silence pervaded the air after those hours of terrific gun-fire. One could still see the flashes across the sky—in imagination!

We went in for a cup of tea and a piece of cake. We would have the bacon *to-day* for breakfast! It was just as I had left it in the pan—but very, very cold!

There are many people, no doubt, who had much more exciting and terrifying experiences than this. But I did my duty, I think (don't you?), and am truly thankful that I and my little family are alive to tell the tale.

9.—FROM A CLIFTONIAN'S DIARY

(By Ubique)

After settling an incendiary which came through the middle gutter of this house while a lady was playing "Patience," I went off on the prowl to see if any assistance was needed in the vicinity. Three doors from here are some stables in which thirteen horses were just finishing their last meal when the blitz "broke."

To my astonishment there was one tethered inside and one outside the gate of this house. Their stable, the church opposite and a chapel at the end of this road in Whiteladies' Road, were blazing away. Having to "back" the one inside and to "gee-gee" the one outside in order to open the gate, I saw the reflection in their eyes, as much as to say: "It looks pretty, but we simply *must* eat all the privet hedges within reach," which they all did thoroughly.

One of the helpers, a lad of about 14, had brought them out of the stable, and had tethered them on both sides of the road. Not one was hurt, or even worried, thanks in part to the privet hedges, now *non est*, alas. This boy, by the way, said he was going to be a "Vet" when he grew up. The following morning the pavements and gutters were covered with manure, to which the garden-lovers helped themselves to renew their privets!

Continuing my prowl I was accosted by a distressed evacuee mother in Aberdeen Road. She asked if I could retrieve the tray with her baby's bottle that she had hurriedly placed on the front lawn. I had a good look, but owing to falling glass from the first floor it was not advisable to approach too near till later. So I informed a fireman and asked the mother to "call again."

Shortly afterwards I observed a fireman nursing what looked like a baby in a white blanket opposite a fire on Whiteladies' Road. I said: "Is the baby hurt?" "What the ——— do you mean? This is our new hose." I evidently had "baby" on the brain! And new hoses they certainly needed, as the old ones were spurting water from punctures from five to ten yards on either side.

In the middle of the pavement opposite the shops above Clifton Down Station I found a "pig-bucket" cover amidst piles of broken glass. It had been used to extinguish an incendiary so I replaced it on the bucket. Further up the road I saw something which I took for a corpse, covered discreetly by a rug. Thinking it was just my unfortunate luck I lifted the rug to see if it was a male or female. It was neither! Just three attache cases and a circular hat box, all carefully labelled. Not a soul was in sight, and only the hissing of leaking hoses in the roadway to be heard.

At St. John's Church I saw two buses, one on each side of the road. Two drivers and two conductors were examining them. A bomb had fallen between them, and they looked as though they had been opened with a giant's tin opener, very roughly, the blue paint and the tin colours contrastingly greatly. The drivers said that they had both disgorged all their passengers and themselves to the near-by shelter in Apsley Road, and none of them were hurt.

There was one extra wonderful performance I must record. A car was lifted from its garage and sent over two houses near Hampton and Abbotsford Roads. It landed right side up, and did not look much the worse. I understand that something of the same kind happened at Westbury-on-Trym.

On a certain day, when I lost my drawing instruments in Prince's Street, I met at the top of Park Street a motor car, evidently going down, with its hind wheels in a hole filled with water; a little lower down was another car, evidently coming up, with its front wheels in a similar hole. No one on their way to business took the slightest notice, all being late as there were no buses.

In a ladies' shop towards the bottom, or was it in the Green? I saw a cat sound asleep on silk underclothing. When spoken to, it said: "I've had a rough night; please do not disturb me." All the glass had been blown outwards, and puss had a soft, warm bed.

I never recovered my drawing instruments, though many plans were saved. They were in a new attache case, but twelve months' afterwards I *did* recover their cost. But it was impossible to replace them at their original cost, as I have, alas! discovered.

P.S. After returning from the prowl above recounted I found an ambulance being loaded up outside a neighbour's house. Two women had sought shelter there, and while waiting to be admitted a bomb fell and buried them, causing their deaths. My neighbour and I had actually been standing on the spot where they lay without being aware that they were beneath our feet.

10—AN INCIDENT IN THE COUNTRY

(MR. R. E. MILNER, " Littlegarth," Leigh Woods)

Incidents in the country are different from those in the city.
There is hardly anyone about, and the few on the roads are hurrying
to get in, or out—some going home, others leaving home to help in
the city.

It was April 11th, 1941, at about 10.30 p.m. We were fire-
watching in the garden of our house at the time. A fire-bomb burst
in the air over the tree tops 50 yards away, and pieces flew off in
all directions.

We thought it was a plane coming down, so bolted for the air-
raid shelter. Just as we had jumped down four H.E's came whistling
to the ground—one only fifty yards away. It made a large crater in
the main road, bursting the water main, and damaging the electric
cable. Another fell in our front garden. It blew away the garden
wall, gate, gate-posts and railings, breaking all the windows and the
roof.

The garden was covered with debris, and the road with large
stones and uprooted trees. A flame 10 ft. high rose from the bottom
of the crater, and we tried to smother it before another raider came
and dropped more bombs. Four times we got sand bags and ran
down the crater, throwing them on the flames, but each time they
came out somewhere else. Then a neighbour arrived with a spade
and shovelled some debris down the bank, and put the fire out.

Two more bombs were dropped in the wood close by ; they
uprooted trees, splitting them from top to bottom, and even hurling
them across the road. Windows and tiles by the hundred were
broken in our neighbours' houses.

As soon as the noise of bursting bombs had subsided, and the
clatter of flying debris and glass ceased, we came up from the shelter
to see what had happened.

We found the whole place lit up with incendiaries; the road was
impassable. Bombs were still coming down in Bristol, and we had
to get busy.

The first thing was to stop the traffic from running into the
crater and debris, so we lit red lights and set them up, rolled the
stones to the side of the road, and made one side of it passable. The
telephone wires were down and a danger, as they stretched across
the road. So we pulled them to the side, only to find that they were
still across the road being fastened at the other side. So we had to
pull them in again on the side they were fastened.

Then we had to let the Electric Light people know that the
cables were hit, the Water people that the main was broken, and also
sent a message to the Police. Meanwhile we stopped some of the
cars by waving handkerchiefs in front of their dimmed headlights.

Inside the house everything was chaotic! Stones, broken glass,
plaster and debris everywhere—and no light! In a downstairs room,
with windows broken, my brother Bernard Milner, well known in

shipping circles in the city, was lying on his death bed, with a sister at each side holding his hands to comfort him. I think nurses and many others who have unflinchingly stuck to their posts attending sick people in heavy air raids have been wonderfully brave, and deserve the highest praise.

In the country on various occasions in our district we have had thousands of incendiary bombs scattered all over the fields and woods. In the darkness it looked like fairyland. One night between Failand and Abbots Leigh about 3,000 were dropped, but the only damage done was a dutch barn, hay rick, and lambing pens burnt.

MY FIRST DAY'S DUTY
(From MR. F. H. DUNN, Thomas Lane, Redcliffe.)

(This experience, occurring as it did when Wine Street stood in all its glory and the old " Dutch House " was its crowning splendour, will recall many memories of that famous street—one of the finest shopping centres in England.—Ed.)

" Early in 1940 I joined up as a Special Constable, and at 2 p.m. one sunny Thursday afternoon I went on my first duty. ' You had better parade Wine Street,' said the Sergeant, and up and down I went in my brand-new uniform, looking, I hope, the part.

" It soon struck me that a policeman is an ' Enquire Within on Everything.' ' Where's the Post Office?' ' Where's the nearest telephone?' ' Which way to the Centre?' etc., etc. In addition I had to keep my eye on the people parking cars to see if they were on the wide portion only, and also to see if they were locked. There were, as usual, crowds of shoppers about.

" Standing at the top of the Pithay a lady came up to me in a fluster. ' Officer,' she said, ' I've just left that shoe-shop, and quite accidentally I threw the bill away down that grating, and a ten-shilling note with it.' Quandary. What to do? Out came my note-book. ' Address, madam, please.' It turned out that she lived in a well-known Bristol vicarage! Next action: Went to street police telephone near grating and rang up the Charge Office to report. Suggested they should get in touch with the Sanitary Depot, Redcliffe. Grating would not budge. Had a look down. It was filled about 4 ·feet down with odd paper, but nothing that looked like a treasury note. Kept cars off my particular grating. Had another brain-wave. Went into boot shop. ' Did they have a stick with a clipper on the end which you use for getting articles from the window?' ' No!'

" The young manager got interested. Suggested some stiff wire off a packing case, and together we went fishing. Picture the scene! A policeman on his first duty looking down the drain with the well-dressed manager lifting out sundry pieces of paper. Very tantalising! They would come up 2 feet and then drop off the wire. But our motto, ' Try, try again,' at last succeeded. Lo and behold up came a ten-shilling note rather wet and soiled. S.C. 240 (that's me) went back to the station triumphant. I'd done my first day's duty."

(Mr. Dunn had *done* it well, too!—Ed.)

PART II.

STORIES OF THE BLITZ

There are said to be only eight quite different themes for a story in the whole world. Whether this be so or not I am not competent to say. But since this literary dictum was propounded a new experience has entered into the world—the experience of being " blitzed!" This makes a ninth theme, and the stories which follow are all variations upon it.

They appear, in the main, as they were received by me. Though it has been necessary to curtail some of them, no essential parts have been omitted. They give an insight of what went on in the homes and streets of the city during the blitzes. Some may make you smile and others may bring a lump to your throat, but all will make you proud of the people. The stories are worth preserving as typical examples of the experiences which befell thousands during those " Siren Nights."

Now that the danger has passed one is apt to sit back in one's chair and smile rather condescendingly at some of the reactions of two years ago. " We made a lot out of trifles," someone said to me not long ago. But when the sirens were sounding and the bombs were dropping there were no trifles! Little things took on a new significance, and the right way to read these stories is for the reader to endeavour to recapture his emotional condition during those harrowing nights.

A number of stories have been culled from the local papers for the sake of completeness. They were too good to have merely an ephemeral existence, and I am grateful for permission to reproduce them in this book.

TEA FOR TWO

(MR. H. LONG, 37, Victoria
Street, Staple Hill.)

Here is an almost perfect
example of the unshakeability
(if such a word exists)—the
absolute refusal to be diverted
from normal ways — of the
average ordinary citizen, and
especially of the older folk.

The circumstances were—
December, 1940; the first
experience of bombs in the
district concerned, and as First
Aid Party Leader I took my
party to the incident. One
bomb had opened the road, and
a gas main was sending a torch

" Indian or China."

to the sky. Two houses were destroyed and many damaged by blast.
There were the usual scenes, with which we later became only too
familiar.

Fortunately the casualties were, in the main, very light. A
number of people from damaged houses had been collected in a basement, and amongst these was an elderly lady who had taken rather
a bad bump, but who was, in fact, mostly suffering from shock.
Knowing that a cup of tea would be useful, I sent my ambulance
attendant upstairs to see if one could be managed. In a surprisingly
short time she returned with a neat tray, and in no time my patient
was gratefully enjoying her refreshment.

Now—the point of the story—my attendant later told me that
the good lady of the house, on the request for tea, immediately pro-
duced the necessary items, set out the tray as for a formal afternoon
caller, and was quite worried as to whether our patient would like
Indian or *China* tea!

Gas main blazing not far away—heavy barrage on—house full of
wardens, messengers, etc.; and *that* was our hostess's only worry—
Indian or China!

THREE CAMEOS

(MRS. M. SYMMONS, 9, Newbury Road, Horfield.)

During one of the heaviest blitz nights my daughter, then aged
12, said to me: " I don't mind dying, mummie, only I wish I was 90
years of age instead of 12." Later on, when we could hardly hear
ourselves speak for noise, she heard some fowls cackling, and said:
" Oh, I do feel sorry for those poor fowls."

I am rather deaf, and seldom hear the sirens. The boy next
door usually knocks me up if there is any danger, with the words:
" You'd better get up. He's droppin' 'em again!"

WHEN A WORM TURNS
(S.P.S.)

An allotment holder who had dug and planted his plot was informed that Jerry had dropped a bomb right in the centre of his garden. He made his way disconsolately to the scene the next day and stood for a while in great dejection on the edge of the gaping crater.

Then he saw a worm carrying on as if nothing had happened. Turning to a sympathetic friend he said: " If that ——— worm can take it, so can I ! " Later on the crater was filled in and the garden replanted.

A NEW USE FOR A STEEL HAT
(S.P.S.)

During a fairly sharp blitz which burst over Brislington a middle-aged lady, of somewhat portly proportions, got her three children, and those of a neighbour, safely beneath her table shelter in the parlour. Then she tried to get in herself, but found it impossible to get her " posterior " under cover.

Seeing her difficulty one of her children passed his steel hat to her, remarking: " Cover it with that, mum! "

THE WHITEHALL WAY
(MR. GERRISH, 91, Gilbert Road, Whitehall, 6.)

On March 16, 1941, Whitehall and Redfield districts were attacked somewhat badly. I was out the whole of the night, and I can vouch for the attention and bravery shown by the fire-party of this district, No. 181. As soon as the bombs started dropping the leader, Mr. Watts, sent parties to assist in all directions, which they did admirably. A bomb fell on four houses opposite to the home of the leader during the night, and the bravery displayed by the party, led by Mr. Watts, to extricate the dead and wounded and administer first aid before the arrival of any other assistance was the most wonderful performance of duty and self-sacrifice I have ever witnessed. I can recommend this as deserving of a place in the pages of your book.

DEVOUTLY TO BE DESIRED
(S.P.S.)

Just outside the south-east corner of Brislington Parish Church is the grave of Thomas Newman, who died at the great age of 153. During one of the raids a H.E. landed right inside the churchyard, perilously near old Thomas's resting place. The following day a villager, looking round, was heard to say: " I'm glad they didn't disturb he, poor old gentleman. All I hope is that Hitler don't live to be as old! "

(Doubt has been expressed as to the accuracy of the age of Newman. But a Mrs. B. Evans, writing in the local press sometime ago, was able to verify it. Her father was a descendant, and the record has been handed down through the generations. Some years ago the stone was re-cut on account of this remarkable age.—Ed.).

A LITTLE MISUNDERSTANDING

(MR. RICH, Sunnyside, Chestnut Road, Long Ashton.)

Before the heavy raids started Bristolians will remember that we had a long series of alerts. When the sirens sounded most people dived to shelter; in fact we wardens were instructed to advise civilians to take shelter. On one occasion, after an alert, the streets were entirely deserted except for one aged citizen. He was standing in the middle of the road, complacently lighting his pipe. I advised him to take cover, but he cupped his hand to his ear and said, " Eh?" After telling him at least six times that the sirens had sounded, it dawned on him what had happened, and he started for the nearest shelter. Before he reached it the All Clear sounded. If I had had a bad ten minutes explaining to the old boy (who was nearly stone deaf) *why* he should go to the shelter, it was nothing to the time I had in trying to tell him why he didn't need to go after all. If he thinks about it at all he probably still thinks, as he did then, that I'm mad!

BRISTOL'S " STARLET "

(From an Open Letter in *John Bull*)

Dear Peggy.—Guns were roaring and bombs dropped near by as you went to sing at Bristol cabaret in aid of soldiers' comforts. It was a heavy " blitz," and you're only twelve, but you carried on till the end. Of course! You've not only talent, but the spirit of your disabled ex-soldier father, who can never work again.

(Peggy Budd is still carrying on her good work. She is one of Bryan Michie's discoveries, and has been described in some national newspapers as a second Gracie Fields.—Ed.)

" HITLER'S COMING "

(S.P.S.)

The scene was a Methodist mission where a prayer meeting was in progress. Unfortunately the suppliants had not been too careful with the black-out, and bright chinks of light shone through the edges of the windows. About this time a blitz was beginning to develop. A few incendiaries had already fallen some distance away, and an auxiliary policeman rushed into the mission room and said: " Put those lights out at once." The leader of the meeting, a veteran Methodist, held up his hand, saying: " Hush! We're calling upon God." " If you don't put those ——— lights out," roared the policeman, " Hitler will soon be calling on you."

" SHE'LL 'BIDE "

(S.P.S.)

It was a beautiful moonlight night. The siren had sounded and a little knot of watchers stood near Hanham Mount, where John Wesley preached to the Kingswood miners two hundred years ago. Bristol lay at their feet, bathed in the light of the moon; no other light was visible—the black-out was complete.

" Well," said one of the watchers, " one thing's certain. ' You can't black out the moon,' as the song says." " No," came an answering voice, in the dialect of the district; " she'll bide! "

A HUMAN BARRAGE

(S.P.S.)

The A-A guns were making a deafening row. A man and his wife in the High Street had gone to bed, and the man was doing his best to get off to sleep. But his wife kept talking about the rattle of the guns and the bursting of the shells.

At last her husband snapped out: " Oh, for goodness sake shut up. How do you expect a fellow to get to sleep when you're making such a row!".

NONCHALANCE

(Mr. E. J. Pollard, 38, Victoria Road, Hanham.)

At the start of a raid a warden of " C Group " was walking along his sector with an A.R.P. messenger when Jerry dropped a flare. The warden remarked to the messenger: " If you happen to look up you will see a flare right above your head, but take no notice." They both calmly kept on patrolling their sector as if the nearest enemy bomber was miles away.

This incident is not very much to read about to-day, perhaps, but during those early raids (before our nerves got settled to such things) it was, I think, very plucky, and worthy of record.

A VISION OF ST. CHAD

(L. Wookey, 26, Mildred Street, Moorfields.)

At a small mission, dedicated to St. Chad, in the Parish of St. Matthew, Moorfield, the congregation were gathered for evensong when the sirens sounded. Guns opened fire and H.E.'s began to fall, but the service carried on.

After the second lesson and before the address the people were given the opportunity of leaving, but most stayed on to the end of the service.

When the doors were opened a lurid glow lit up the city. All went home except ten, who remained in the mission until 11.40 p.m., ducking under seats when sounds of bombs passed overhead or explosions occurred in the vicinity.

Prayers were said, and the hymn, " Lord keep us safe this night " was sung as we had never sung it before. The Lay Reader kept up the spirit of the people splendidly, and when the blitz was over he dismissed the remnant of the congregation.

He arrived home to find that a bomb had destroyed four houses opposite his own, with only the loss of one life, that of a little boy who was in the shelter with his mother and father. Many of the people in his street had wonderful escapes, and the Lay Reader's house was practically undamaged.

While walking home his wife saw a vision of a protecting angel by their sides as they stepped over piles of broken glass and debris in the street.

Was it the spirit of their Patron Saint? I know what we think!

38

HOW THE CHILDREN "TOOK IT!"
(Miss Wensley, 48, Zetland Road, Redland.)

I think we have not all of us realised the terrific courage of the children during the raids, so I am sending one or two stories from my own experience. To one who had to sit in shelters with them and watch (knowing how helpless one was) their pluck was an example to the adults.

On one occasion I was in charge of 50 children (the youngest $3\frac{1}{2}$ and the eldest $5\frac{1}{2}$) when, with no warning, a bomb fell just near, rocking the building to its foundations. This was followed by the wail of sirens, and we ran, in perfect order, to an outdoor shelter, with gunfire around and above us. Panting and dishevelled we sat down on the hard forms—when "Donald" looked around him and remarked in a disgusted voice: "Well, if I'd known *this* was going to happen I'd have brought my pear to eat whilst I was here waiting." In that moment the tension and fear were lifted and gone.

" Their voices never faltered."

In my own shelter on another occasion 30 of us, still children under 6 (except my "helper," who was 8), experienced Bristol's first great daylight raid. We had been having solos by varied children when the guns became so very loud (and remember we had never really heard them before) that I decided that community singing was our best remedy. For half-an-hour we raised the roof with every popular song we knew, going back over them again and again rather than pause for a second. In that thirty minutes—which seemed like a century—I watched 30 little faces go whiter and whiter, and 30 pairs of eyes fill with horror and fear. But their little voices never faltered —no one cried or called out. They grinned as they sang right to the bitter end. We went home speechless from our efforts, but we'd seen that first daylight raid through, and we had learned how Bristol children could and would " take it."

(We have learned, too, how Bristol teachers could " take it."—Ed.)

" SAVE ME THE FIN "
(Mrs. Hill, 5, Lyndale Avenue, Stoke Bishop.)

H.E.'s and incendiaries had just fallen; father was dashing to put out one of the latter in the garden, when from the shelter came the voice of young son: " Dad, save me the fin!"

SACRAMENT AND SACRIFICE
(S.P.S.)

A young soldier, attached to the Bomb Disposal Squad remained for Holy Communion at a Sunday mid-day celebration at Brislington Parish Church. It was his first communion there. A few hours later he made the great sacrifice, being killed by blast while helping to evacuate the inmates of a maternity home in Hampstead Road, though off duty!

A TALL ORDER
(R. D. PAULL, F.A. Depot, No. 3, Warmley.)

Having been on all night (16/3/41) without any rest and no drink or food, and no likelihood of getting any, I asked my party driver to go and fetch something to eat, and try to get some water so that we could have a cup of tea. This was at 6.30 a.m., and at 7.15 he returned with a kettle of water and some eatables, but we had to return to our depot at Soundwell Clinic First Aid Post immediately, and so missed these good things. No sooner had we arrived than we were ordered to another part of the city—St. Andrew's Park. The usual sights of destruction and mess met our eyes. Having rendered what assistance we could, we were collecting our things to return to our depot when all at once the head of an old lady appeared at what was once a window. She called out to us and we went to see what the trouble was. " Could you please get my windows put in," she called, " and repair the water main for me at once?" Well, we had done most things that night, but putting windows in was a little beyond us at the time. When we asked about the water we found that the old lady was dying for a cup of tea. So to finish off the night we gave her the kettle of water that the car driver had secured with so much difficulty, and left her very happy. But it was a long time before we got our cup of tea.

THE STORY OF " PRINCE "
(Anon.)

This is the story of " Prince," the dog who wouldn't die.

A few months before the blitz on March 16th, 1941, his owner contemplated having him destroyed, but on consideration he reprieved him and gave him to Mr. Nelson Woodhams. He was taken to the Animal Dispensary, and the vet., after careful examination, declared him to be " worth another chance."

On the night of the above-mentioned blitz the whole rank of houses, in one of which " Prince " lived, collapsed, burying him under the debris. No trace of him was to be found until nearly a fortnight afterwards (all but four hours), when a demolition squad, detailed to work on the site, dug him out alive!

It is pathetic to record that his previous owner, who thought " Prince " not fit to live, was himself killed on the same night, in an attempt to return to his house to extinguish some incendiaries.

40

A NARROW SHAVE.

(Mr. R. E. Martin, 31, Seymour Avenue, Bristol, 7.)

I was attached to the Richmond Road Fire Party, Section 2 (Montpelier), and on March 16th, 1941, was standing with two other watchers when Jerry dropped a flare. I was between the other two, just about a yard apart, when suddenly I heard a rush of air (like an express train) coming. " Look out! " I shouted, and crouched down as low as I could against a pillar. Down the bomb came, landing just beside my honeysuckles. I felt the heat of the detonation and this blew me around the corner of a pillar. Then followed the blast which took me right through a passage, tearing off the soles of my shoes and ripping my overcoat to shreds. Both my colleagues were killed, as were eleven others, and four substantial houses were destroyed. My own home was totally wrecked, but why was I spared? That is what I kept asking myself during 14 weeks at the B.R.I. Perhaps it will be revealed to me later. Had I lain down, I should never have got up alive!

LIGHTS OUT!

(Anon.)

During a heavy raid on the city, in which Ashton Gate was hit pretty badly, the occupants of two houses in Smythe Road were away on A.R.P. duty in the city, and both houses were locked. An incendiary fell through the roof into a bedroom of one of the houses, and owing to the black-out the fire was not immediately seen.

After fruitless efforts with the stirrup pump we decided to break into the adjacent house, although the flames were leaping some 10 to 15 feet from the roof. We managed to do this, switched on the lights in order to see what we were doing, and started getting the furniture out, although bombs were falling all over the place. In the midst of these operations we heard the stentorian voice of a zealous warden shouting: " Put those ——— lights out! "

" FOUR FARTHINGS—ONE PENNY "

(Mr. W. T. H. Gill, St. Denis, Channel View, Portishead.)

The following incident is worthy of notice as an example of the English way of taking difficulties.

On the night of the Good Friday blitz (1941) my house at Portishead was partially destroyed by a bomb. At the time my housekeeper had her aunt, who was 73 years old, staying with her. Her name was Farthing, and she had already been bombed out in her Bristol home. She was pinned under the wreckage of our house with a broken ankle. When the rescue party had released her, they asked her her name, and she replied, with a smile: " Four farthings—one penny."

During the same raid I myself was buried under the house. I remember the relief I felt when what I thought was a huge piece of masonry about to crush me turned out to be the cushion of a reclining chair.

AN EXPECTANT MOTHER

(MR. E. J. POLLARD, 38, Victoria Road, Hanham.)

Mr. Sparks, of Barrow Road, tells of three women who were in a shelter in a back garden during a raid in his district. Three incendiaries dropped into the garden, and one of the women immediately left the shelter and covered the bombs with sand, successfully. It was a wonderful deed, as she was an expectant mother, and gave birth to a child fourteen days after.

THE CANARY KEPT ON SINGING

(Anon.)

A bomb crashed through a house at Kingswood, bringing it to the ground in ruins, and killing the two inmates. As the rescue party set to work they were surprised to hear the song of a bird beneath the debris. Guided by the song they discovered a cage, partly flattened out, within which was a canary, unhurt, and apparently undisturbed. It sang defiance to Hitler!

STAYED WITH THE DOG

(MR. E. J. POLLARD, 38, Victoria Road, Hanham.)

During the Good Friday raid (1941) a lady and her two daughters, residing at Hanham, were invited to go to a friend's shelter. The two girls asked if they could take their dog. Their mother said: " No, of course not." So the girls (aged 10 and 12) absolutely refused to go to the shelter and forsake their pet. A beautiful illustration of " Love me love my dog."

THE DOCTOR " MAKES " IT

(SILENT WITNESS, 1, Florence Place, Southville.)

At the height of the blitz on Good Friday (1941) it fell to my luck to help a doctor get his car started, after his garage had taken a blasting. It started, and we got into the roadway. Allington Road was blocked each end. Efforts to remove fallen masonry were useless, so he drove his car over the rubble like a tank. Two beauties burst in the vicinity. But that gentleman got to the casualty station that night. *More* than luck was on his side!

" R."

(MR. G. P. HULME, 117, Coldharbour Road, Redland.)

The district was Bedminster: the time—the " day after "; the scene: working-class houses totally demolished, several large craters in amongst them. Stuck on the top of a 6-feet wall (all that remained of a very high one) was one of those letter " Rs " (repairs) for putting in windows. A spot of humour amidst desolation—something bright and funny set against a background of wreckage and pathos.

SIR ADRIAN DID'NT BOLT

("EVENING WORLD" DIARY, 13/5/43.)

The B.B.C. Symphony Orchestra found itself faced with all sorts of difficulties soon after setting up its first war base at Bristol. There was the epic occasion when, contributing to an epilogue under fire, Paul Beard played Bach's Air on the G String while kneeling on the floor of a tiny studio, and Stuart Hibberd broadcast the reading from Scripture while sheltering with the microphone under the table. But whatever the Luftwaffe did over the heads of the famous orchestra, it never made Adrian bolt. He stuck to his guns—or rather his baton—through it all, and so did his colleagues.

The story of the prudence of the driver of the instrument van one night when bombs were falling and fires burning deserves to be recorded in these pages. Instead of taking the van to the garage he drove it out into the country, and there guarded the instruments through the night. When he drove back to the garage in the morning he found that a bomb had wrecked it.

FORCE OF HABIT

(MISS ROWLES, 80, Coleford Road, Southmead.)

When we were bombed out, my mother and I were under the stairs, and we had a Providential escape. Neither of us was hurt, though all but the outside walls came down all around us. There were also two other houses attached to ours, and one of the ladies who lived next to us, who had gone to a shelter, had the surprise of her life when the raid was over. When she left the shelter she crossed the road to where part of her house was standing, went straight to her door (or what ought to have been her door), took her key from her handbag, and placed it into—nothingness! There was no door—only the shell of what used to be her home.

At the time we were all too dazed to see the funny side of this incident, but now, whenever we meet our old neighbour, we have a good laugh at the way she tried to open a door that wasn't there.

PLUCKY GIRLS

(MR. L. SHIELD, 5, Maurice Road, St. Andrew's Park.)

During the Bath blitz of April, 1942, a party of workers set out from the A.R.P. Centre to render what help they could. When they reached Saltford they were spotted by Jerry, who immediately started machine-gunning them.

They took what shelter they could, ultimately arriving at Bath, where they carried out their work of mercy among the sufferers. The young full-time A.R.P. worker in charge of this rescue party has spoken very highly of the way in which the girls performed every duty assigned to them. It was not until after their return that any sign was given of the strain which all this had meant to them.

THE BEETROOT

(MRS. ALLEN, 87 Greenbank Road, Easton)

My daughter and I were under the stairs one terrible night for 11 hours. Every minute we thought we simply must go. In fact I kept my head under my girl's arm, saying, " If we have to go we'll go together." During a lull in the bombing my daughter said she was hungry, so we left our place of refuge and went into the back room. On the table were some beetroots, and I picked one up, saying: " I'd love to shoot a beetroot right into Jerry's eye so that he would miss the way."

He might have heard me, for the next moment there was a terrific crash. All the glass was blown out of the window, and I rushed back to our glory-hole still holding on to the beetroot. When the raid was over *we* had it, instead of Jerry.

A BAKER-HERO

(MRS. OSBORNE, 40 Kennington Avenue, Bishopston)

On the night of Nov. 24th, 1940, my husband's father, Albert James Osborne, of Knowle, was preparing to go to his work when the first big raid on Bristol commenced. He was a baker by trade and so worked by night. His son, with whom he was living, begged him to wait as the district was being heavily attacked, and many fires were already raging. But he insisted on going, saying: " People will want their bread to-morrow, whatever happens to-night."

He went out, but never reached his work. He was killed by a bomb as he went to bake the people's bread; his sons found his body two days later in the General Hospital mortuary. I feel that he gave his life for his fellow-men as surely as if he had died on the battle-field. This is only one of the many brave, but unrecognised deeds, that were performed during those ghastly nights.

SONGS IN THE NIGHT

(Evening World)

At a Bristol hospital during the raid in January, 1941, men patients sang while the raid was at its height in order to calm the nerves of the women patients. They were joined by the nursing staff, who worked under the greatest difficulties with the calmness and cheerfulness that won the praise of their Matron, Miss Seth-Smith, who herself conducted the work with the utmost *sangfroid*.

A bomb which fell early in the evening, exploded with such force that nurses were blown off their feet, and one man patient was lifted bodily from his bed on to that of another in the same room. " The nurses worked like bricks," said the Matron, " and with the greatest cheerfulness and willingness."

FAGGED OUT

(MRS. FARE, 113 Ashton Drive, Ashton Vale)

My sister was a warden all through the blitzes. On January 3rd, 1941, an incendiary fell through the roof of a house near which my sister was standing. She raced across to the house and found the inmates playing a game. "There's an incendiary upstairs," she shouted. They at once started to remove the furniture, but my sister said: "Leave all that. It's upstairs," and she ran up to the room where it was. It had gone clean through the bed, and was burning its way through the floor.

She could find no sand, water, or earth, so ran outside and started scratching up some earth from the frozen ground with her finger nails. Then she crawled under the bed and was just going

" Toiling with the salvage party."

to throw the earth on the bomb when " Swish!" A bucket of water landed right in her face. A man had heard cries for water, and filled a bucket; knowing the bomb was under the bed he rushed upstairs and flung the icy water on it without realising that my sister was there. The water froze on her face and legs!

Shortly after the "All Clear" we heard that our old home in Bedminster was partially demolished. A bomb had fallen in my aunt's garden and swept half the street away. My sister and I, without having any rest, went at once to Stafford Street, Mill Lane, there to find chaos. We worked all the Saturday until nearly tea-time, toiling with a salvage party, to get away as much as we could from what was once our home.

We were too tired to eat, and my sister, still with her helmet on leaned back in the chair and went off to sleep. Half an hour later, at 6.15 p.m., the sirens sounded again, but my sister was dead asleep. The wardens were blowing their whistles, but we couldn't make her understand. She was just too fagged out, and slept until nine o'clock. Then she woke up, and went straight off to do her duty again!

(This warden was highly commended in a report for her utter disregard for her personal safety, and is now a war-time worker.—Ed.)

THE BROGUE

(MISS COLLEY, 46 Lloyd Road, Northampton)

Two friends of mine, returning to London, have got an old Irish charwoman who had worked for them in happier days in Bristol. Soon after their return the charwoman, who remained in Bristol, had her little home blown to bits in an air raid. Hearing of her plight, they asked her to go and live with them in London.

She jumped at the offer, and the first thing she said when she arrived was: " Shure, in the big blitz, I lost everything I ever possessed—except me brogue! " And she is still working away, briskly, accompanied by her brogue.

A CHILD'S PRAYER

(MRS. MELKINS, 46 Bayham Road, Knowle)

During a very bad raid we were sitting under the stairs when a house a few feet away had a direct hit, dividing it in half. When the raid was over we went to the front door and looked out. I remarked to my children and grandson that I really didn't know why we were spared. " I do, Gran," said my grandson. " I've been praying all the time the raid has been on, that God would spare us, so that I could see my Dad and Mum again." I may add that his Dad is in the forces, and was in France during the capitulation.

(There were many stories of this kind received, and we feel one ought to be recorded.—Ed.).

SPIRIT OF YOUTH

(MR. C. PRICE, 70 Park Road, Staple Hill)

On the Sunday night of the first blitz, I was one of ten beneath a table for six hours. When the " All Clear " sounded we went into the street, viewing the wreckage. A girl of 17, with helmet and mask, was pointed out to me. She had been at her post (a telephone) through the whole night—alone! All through this night members of the local lad's club were incessantly working putting out bombs, fires, getting people to safety, and rescuing others from wrecked houses.

JACK TARS HELP

(*Evening World,* November 27th, 1940)

Two "Jolly Jack Tars" have their names posted up at one of the A.F.S. Stations as an acknowledgment of the help they gave the firemen.

"We were just about beaten," said one A.F.S. man, "when we saw two Jolly Jack Tars coming along Queen's Road. Neither they nor we knew how they got there, because they were on their way to some other place. They came along just as we were staggering with a hose, and said: "Let's have a go at it, pals." They had never held a hose before, but as there was not full pressure at this spot it was not too difficult. Suddenly, however, the water came out at full pressure. The sailors reeled—not Jack Tar fashion—and turned the hose on themselves. They struggled up, however, went swaying across the road, and turned the pipe on the spot where it would do most good. They were stout fellows, and worked like Trojans all the night. After an hour's sleep at the station, they continued their journey."

QUICK WORK

(Miss M. Fagnani, 52 Colston Street)

A delayed action bomb landed at the bottom of Christmas Steps during the Good Friday blitz. The week following the dustmen were standing arguing at the top of the Steps as to whether they should go and collect the rubbish which the inhabitants had sneaked down and put out ready for them. They kept looking at the danger notice, and finally decided that they weren't going to risk their lives. So I said to them: "Nonsense. Not only have we been bombed, but we shall be gassed as well if that stuff is left for another week. I'll go and get it for you."

This must have shamed them a little, because they altered their minds and emptied the dustbin. But I never saw refuse cleared away so swiftly. All records must have been broken that morning.

GOOD OUT OF EVIL

(Miss M. Fagnani, 52 Colston Street)

A knock came at the door of a house near Christmas Steps during the height of the first blitz in November 1940. When it was opened a relative was standing there who had not been seen for eight years, owing to a family misunderstanding. He had come from Horfield direction, from where he could see the bright glow from the burning city.

He said to his friends: "My people are down there amidst all that. I *must* go to them." It was a happy reunion; all the awful bitterness of years was wiped out, so once again, "Out of evil cometh good!"

BLIND LEADING THE BLIND
(Anon.)

The sirens were giving their warning full blast, and on my way to the shelter I knocked my eye on the branch of a tree and could hardly see a thing. Afterwards on arriving near home I saw an old lady striking matches in the street, trying to find her way in the dark. I had a small torch and took her to the address she wanted, and discovered as we went along that she, too, had only got the use of one eye.

LAUGHTER AND TEARS
(MRS. WESTON, 499 Gloucester Road, Horfield)

This is typical of many letters received.

" I lived in St. Nicholas Road, St. Paul's, and I well remember the bad raid in Dean Street, in December, 1940. My father and mother were bombed out, also my husband's family, so they came and stayed with my husband and me and our three boys. That meant ten of us in a five-roomed house. I had no light or water, so we had to cook in an oven grate in the room some of us slept in. We all had a good laugh when we thought of my old dad (81), who had been blown amongst the coal and who took a bit of scrubbing to get clean again. Also my mother-in-law, who took in washing, made us laugh when she described how a sailor made a dive for her washing and rescued it from being wrecked.

" In the new year (1941) they managed to get a house, and I evacuated my two young boys to Devon with Newfoundland Road School. On March 16th there was another blitz. At its worst my boy and I were in a neighbour's shelter, whilst my husband was helping to put out incendiaries. Suddenly a H.E. hit a corner shop, and also my husband. My boy rushed out to his father whilst I tried to find someone with a car. We could not have the ambulance as it was waiting to take the people to the hospital who were buried beneath the shop. But they did not need it, for all seven of them were killed. The bombs were dropping and the guns were firing, but my boy would not leave his dad. A sailor helped to lift him in a small car, and my boy and I held him, terribly injured, all the way to the hospital.

" I class my boy at sixteen, a hero; he would not leave my side all through that terrible journey. My husband died a few days after, and my son, now eighteen, has joined up. His last word to me before he went, was: ' I'm taking up where dad left off '."

TALE WITH A MORAL
(Evening World)

A sea-captain who had lost his last ship by enemy action was at home when the first raid started. He and his wife had just had dinner, and he said: " I'll help you to wash up before we go to the shelter."

As they were so engaged, a bomb hit the house and demolished every bit except the kitchen! Moral: Help your wife.

THE " DEAD MAN " RAN
(Anon.)

During one of the blitzes, two houses in the street in which I live were set alight. After putting out the fires we were making our way back to my wife and children who were sheltering under the stairs, when a H.E. screamed down. At that time we hadn't got used to them, but experience told us afterwards that H.E.s that make a noise are not intended for you. The ones you can hardly hear are yours.

When this particular H.E. screamed down, I dived for an open doorway, and when I came out again a woman from the opposite side of the street screamed that a man was dead on the pavement. I looked round, and true enough there *was* a man on the pavement. I bent down to pick him up, when down screamed another H.E. I made a dash for my doorway, but someone else was dashing with me. It was the " dead man," and my word—he could run! He'd just been lying flat, like most of us did when H.E.s fell, and was too scared to get up. That was all!

A TALE OF SPUDS
(Anon.)

A man who had a garden on the steepest part of Conham Hill, St. George, delayed digging up his potatoes, of which he had a goodly crop. One night Jerry dropped a bomb among his spuds, sweeping away every vestige of his labours. Not a sign of a potato could be seen; even the shallow earth had been scattered to the four winds, revealing the rock beneath.

The next day one of the oldest inhabitants stood in a small crowd surveying the scene. " Serves the old . . . . right," was his only comment. " I told 'im to dig un up only yesterday night."

"WATER, WATER EVERYWHERE, BUT . . . ."
(*Evening World*)

An A.F.S. man, walking with an empty bucket in his hand, said to a passer-by: " For eighteen hours I've been pumping thousands of gallons of water on a fire, and now, when I come off duty, I have to go and beg a bucketful of water before I can have a shave!"

COMMUNITY OF TWO
(*Evening Post*)

During one of the worst blitzes, a Clifton lady was sheltering in a cupboard with her maid, who was inclined to be jittery. Her mistress sought to fortify her with wise counsel and a little stimulant. This evidently had a beneficial effect, for after a few minutes the girl said: " Don't you think we might try a little community singing, mum?"

NO BOMB CAN STOP HIS SMILE

(MRS. HUNT, 6 Kenmare Road, Knowle Estate)

Mrs. Winston Churchill has seen a letter which Bobby Hunt, aged 11, of Bristol, sent to his mother, saying: " I am keeping my smile." And that was a wonderful thing to do, because Bobbie wrote that letter after he had been bombed out of three hospitals. The letter Mrs. Churchill saw was the one Bobbie wrote while convalescing at Weston-super-Mare, in which he said: " I should think everyone in Bristol had a rough time. Never mind, it will not break our spirits, will it?"

In the first hospital, recovering from rheumatic fever, Bobbie was carried from the third floor to a second floor corridor when the bombing started. Then the side of the building was blown in. As the doctor was carrying him out of the hospital, a rain of incendiaries and H.E.s came down. The doctor laid him under the hedge until he could be placed in a motor-coach. When he got to the second hospital a bomb shattered all the glass. They sent him to a third hospital, and bombs fell nearby. It was then he wrote his letter mentioned above. He kept his word. Still smiling he has now returned to school.

PROGNOSTICATION!

(MRS. OLIVER, St. Nicholas Road, St. Paul's)

After the Good Friday blitz I went to bed at 3 a.m., but was unable to sleep. I had a feeling that something was wrong. So I went upstairs, and *there* was a great paving stone swaying on a broken beam. If it had fallen it would have killed my husband, who was asleep downstairs. I at once woke him up, and he went on the roof with some ropes, and was able to remove the flag-stone the same way that it got in. It is used for covering our shelter.

BENEATH THE STAIRS

(MR. A. SIMMONDS, St. Andrew's Road, Avonmouth)

Though I had travelled all over the world during my seafaring experience and weathered many a storm, though I had been twice torpedoed and been under shell-fire from enemy submarines and suffered from frost-bite owing to exposure in open boats, yet I maintain that the blitz on Avonmouth, on January 16-17, 1941, was easily my biggest nightmare. During that blitz, my wife and married daughter and grandchild—a mere babe—were with me under the stairs. Outside it was as if brimstone and fire were falling from heaven. What touched me most was that the baby knew as if by instinct that something was wrong, and clutched my fore-finger each time a bomb fell. And there we stayed, as did thousands of others, huddled together under the stairs, expecting death or injury every moment, until the All Clear. I have since done a voyage to sea and back again in convoy without incident!

THE CANARY STUCK IT

(Mr. F. Whitlock, 1 Vauxhall Villas, Ashton Gate)

Mr. Whitlock, who was re-siding at Gladstone Street, Bedminster, tells of the terrible night of January 3-4, 1941. He and his family and some friends were crowded into a shelter, which, though full, was made to accommodate a lonely old lady. Had she not found shelter there she would have had to stay at home. Her house was down flat by the morning! It was a lively night. Bombs fell all around, and in between the explosions was heard the tinkling of broken glass. Those

"*In flew the canary.*"

in the shelter kept up their spirits by chiding each other that his or her window had gone west, and they would have a draughty bed-room to sleep in when the raid was over.

The house opposite was swept away, and two soldiers and two civilians, passers-by at an unlucky moment, were swept away too. Fires were everywhere, and eleven people who were fighting one fire all perished. In the shelter they longed for daylight, for they had been shaken about like a pack of cards many times by falling bombs, which sounded like cracks of a whip, only a thousand times worse. At long last the "All Clear" went. I had a look in the parlour and found that two partition walls had collapsed; the bird's cage was still hanging on another wall with the door wide open and the door of the room wide open too. But there was no canary. About an hour later, during an improvised breakfast, in flew the canary. How that relieved our feelings by giving us a good laugh!

SAVING ST. MATTHEW'S, MOORFIELDS

(Mr. W. G. Pope, 18 Cowper Street, Redfield)

During one of the blitzes, an incendiary fell on the roof of this church, and would most certainly have destroyed it but for the efforts of fire-watchers in the neighbourhood. Climbing to the roof on ladders which were available, these watchers, men and women, fought the fire with stirrup pumps and buckets. Three times the fire was thought to have been extinguished, but again it burst into flames, until at last the fire-parties overcame it. All this time H.E.s were falling on buildings on both sides of the road, a large fire at the nearby Co-op. giving the attackers their bearings. This was a fine example of response to a call in time of need.

" WHA' 'I' OI' ? "

(Mr. J. T. Goss, 174 Gloucester Road)

When incendiaries fell in a certain sector of Gloucester Road on Good Friday, 1941, smoke was seen coming from a window above an unoccupied shop. The Fire Party Leader and a companion climbed up to the room to investigate. Meanwhile the N.F.S. arrived on the scene, and a fireman promptly entered the shop, a colleague going to the room overhead.

Observing smoke coming through a hole in the ceiling of the shop, the first fireman struck at it with his hatchet. Unknown to him his colleague was crawling on the floor above, trying to find the incendiary. The result was he got a sharp blow on the jaw from below and was knocked out.

" Take n' ou'," said the leader to his pal. " 'E'll be aw righ' i' th' open air.' As he stooped to lift him up, the prostrate fireman began to show signs of recovering. He blinked his eyes, and said: " Wha' 'i' oi'?" Students of Bristol dialect will recognise that he was simply asking what had hit him! He soon recovered, and was able to carry on, treating the whole thing as a good joke.

A MUCH HIT CONVENT

(*Evening World*)

Schoolgirls and nuns ran from their shelter to deal with incendiary bombs which had fallen on their convent, and succeeded in putting out many. They also carried furniture and other property from that part of the convent which was in danger. A young helper, Desmond Burgess, borrowed a tin hat, and went with his father to give a hand in fighting the flames. He stayed there all night, and was actually on duty for 14 hours. One of the nuns described his courage as " magnificent." This convent has suffered from air raid damage four times.

CATS AND DOGS

(*Western Daily Press*)

In a vicious air raid on the city, a fire started in the premises adjoining the Dogs' Home. The front doors of the house were blistered, and the boarding-kennels were alight. The boiler-house doors were burning, and the cats' quarters were full of smoke. Mr. C. W. Raymond, the head keeper, rescued eleven cats from their quarters, and then attended to the dogs, between 50 and 60 of them, all frantic. He removed the boarders from the blazing kennels to the safe side of the Home, while bombs were dropping, and then released some twenty dogs, which were uncontrollable with fright. Not one animal was injured. Mr. Raymond received the R.S.P.C.A. Silver Medal for his splendid action. Similar medals have been awarded to Inspectors F. Steele, W. K. Fordham and F. Horner for risking their own lives during air raids to save the lives of animals.

LEVITATION !

(Evening World)

A Bristol doctor was in his house during a raid in December, 1940, when it received a direct hit. The next thing seen of him was when he was found in the hall of another house parallel with his own. He was carried there by blast, and had passed through two windows.

When discovered he was so black that he closely resembled a negro. It was as such that he was received into the B.R.I., and it was only when he was bathed that the nurse recognised him as an Hon. Member of the Staff!

JUST LIKE THE FILMS

(Evening World)

The day after the Bristol children arrived at their billets in the Exeter area, a little girl came to one of the escorts and said: " Oh, miss! I have a lovely home, just like the films, and a glass door opens on a piece of grass." Then she continued, excitedly: " And there's a servant, and the lady said: ' Don't run. into the kitchen if you want anything. Ring the bell and the maid will come.' I tried it—and she *came*! Isn't it lovely?"

" A BIT CHILLY "

(Evening Post)

Twenty-year-old Percy Smith recounts this story of what befell him on the night of January 3rd, 1941. " I was walking along by the canal when I heard a shout from a man who was standing on the landing-stage on the other side. He yelled: ' Get this barge shifted!' The barge was loaded with barrels of tar, and was threatened by flames from premises which were burning behind it.

" I threw off my coat and dived into the canal in my shirt and trousers, and came back with a long tow-rope. Some more men then helped to tow the barge across, and we moored it where it would be safe. It *was* a bit chilly!"

SUFFER THE LITTLE CHILDREN

(Western Daily Press)

" When a bomb fell through the roof of the operating theatre at the Children's Hospital," said Staff Nurse Dingle, " there was a deafening crash. I found a window-frame around my neck, and we were all a little dazed. But our Matron, Miss Ellis, was wonderful. ' We must get the children out of here,' she said.

" So we set to work, and picked up as many children as we could carry and ran with them into the road. We were lucky enough to get a bus and army lorry to take us all to another hospital about a quarter of a mile away. The kiddies behaved splendidly. They were quite cheerful, and one tiny tot of between four and five, was singing: ' Roll out the barrel,' as the bombs were falling."

THE WALLS GOT TIRED

(MR. J. J. REYNOLDS, 2 Nova Scotia Place, Bristol)

The second blitz night in Bristol! May and Hassells timber yards well alight, and a little widow in her cottage right in the path of the flames. Across the water were ten or more men, young and old, interested in watching the blaze. Suddenly someone thinks of the widow's cottage, and immediately they made their way to it.

Everything, almost, was removed in record time, and as the last of her things came out, the walls of her cottage got tired and just laid down in one heap. But that boy out East was rather surprised to know he had another address to write to to find his dear old mother.

CHILDREN'S BODY-GUARD

(Evening Post)

" We are thanking God we are alive at the moment," said the Secretary of a Bristol hospital after a raid in 1941. " The nurses were magnificent; they threw themselves on the top of children to protect them as they heard the whistle of the bomb." A sister at the same hospital said that the kiddies took it very well, but she could not speak too highly of the Staff, most of whom were girls of 18!

" No words could express their coolness and bravery in such a terrifying experience," she added. " First the lights failed, and we lit the night-lights. Then came the explosion that put them all out, and we were in darkness save for those of us who had torches. We had to be careful in our use of these lest we showed a light, the windows all being out. How we got out I shall never be able to say." Two men doctors and one lady doctor were in the hospital at the time, and they were marvellous in their leadership.

CAN WE DO YOU NOW, SIR ?

(Evening World)

When incendiaries set fire to some business premises in the City during the first blitz, ten charwomen, who were waiting to commence work in a building nearby, were told to take shelter. " Not on yer life, sir," was the reply to the Head of the Department.

They emptied the coal buckets they had been carrying, filled them with water, and formed a water-bucket chain to the Home Guard men who were fighting the flames. Though working under a glass-covered corridor through which anti-aircraft shell fragments were crashing, they kept the water supply going, assisted by three night watchmen. As a result of their gallant conduct, the premises in which they were working were saved.

(They did their stuff well enough to satisfy even Tommy Handley!—Ed.).

NOT SO FEMININE AFTER ALL

(Western Daily Press)

This is a pleasant little tale. In a Bristol boarding house lived a pale, anæmic, self-conscious youth, pitied and a little despised by his fellow boarders. But this boy, previously regarded as a "bit feminine," was out-of-doors to lend a hand as soon as the blitz of January 3rd, 1941 began.

A three-storey house had collapsed trapping people beneath it. With another man this despised youth sawed through a massive oak beam, and then crouched for half-an-hour supporting the beam on his shoulders whilst rescue parties were feverishly working to release the victims, bombs falling all the time.

(A fine example of the powers which lie latent in the most—apparently—unpromising people—Ed.).

JULIANA

(Western Daily Press)

Juliana was a four-year-old Great Dane when this incident happened. Her master is Mr. W. T. Britton, of Brentry, and during a raid on the City, Juliana discovered an incendiary bomb, smothered it, and thus prevented serious damage to one of her master's premises, a boot repairer's shop in the City area. The Great Dane spent most of her time at the shop, and was there one night with the fire-fighters when a heavy raid developed. While the watchers were dealing with some fires nearby, an incendiary fell, unknown to them, into a room at the back of the shop. But Juliana knew about it. Showing no signs of distress, she provided the evidence that she had put "paid" to the bomb by the burns on her face, claws and pads, and scorched whiskers. While clawing at the damaged door, probably trying to break through to get help, she put out the fire and smothered the incendiary by jumping on it!

LADY DOCTOR'S PLUCK

(Evening World)

Dr. Ann Craig, in charge of a suburban health centre, helped to save the building from destruction. She was at the clinic when the raid started, and shortly afterwards the "thud" of incendiaries could be heard all around.

The doctor ran out of the clinic, climbed on to a pile of sand-bags protecting one of the clinic windows, and from the top of these she gained the roof of the building where a number of incendiaries were burning. Other volunteers (A.R.P.) followed her example, and it was only by their prompt action that the clinic was saved.

DEAD RIGHT

(Evening World)

An energetic, lively old gentleman came up to a street fire-fighting party as the guns began their summer lightning in the darkened skies. Suddenly there was a stutter of machine-gun fire far away.

"That's a fighter," said the stranger. "Listen! He's got him," said the stranger, again. "His engine's faltering. He's falling!"

The fire-fighting party listened hard, but heard nothing.

"He's crashed! He's got him I tell you," continued the old gentleman. "Listen!" But nothing was heard by the F.P.

Then a sudden glow lit the distant sky. A moment—and it was gone. "That's him," said the stranger. "He's down. Good-night!"

And off he trotted into the night, and the curious part of this story is that he was dead right!

ANGUS

(Western Daily Press)

Angus was a three-year-old Scottie, belonging to Mrs. T. Cottle, and was a hero of the blitz. He warned his mistress, who was 67 and very deaf, that an incendiary had fallen on her house, and he was mainly responsible for saving the house and probably her life.

"I had taken shelter under the stairs," said Mrs. Cottle, "taking my little dog with me as I usually did. As I am deaf I could not hear much of the noise that was going on. Suddenly Angus began to bark and growl, and was obviously so distressed that I came out from under the stairs to find out what was the matter. Upstairs I found that an incendiary had fallen through the roof, and had burned the ceiling of my bedroom, setting fire to the carpet. I did not feel capable of dealing with the bomb myself, so I ran into the street and called the fire-watchers, who got it out in no time." This was in April, 1941.

MYSTERY HOLES

(Western Daily Press)

During a raid in the December of 1940 two incendiaries fell on the grass verge of a road, and began to burn brilliantly. There passed that way a young girl who, with British nonchalance, dug up some earth with a stick, piled the earth on the bombs, extinguished them, and went calmly home.

Some time afterwards a man walked along that road, saw the holes where the earth had been dug, and jumped to the not unnatural conclusion that unexploded bombs were about. The matter was reported and there was even talk of evacuation, until A.R.P. experts came along and solved the mystery of the holes.

BANG, BANG, BANG

(Western Daily Press)

During an air raid warning certain residents were aroused by the sound of near-by explosions. This happened during a quiet hour in the night watches, but the ever-alert wardens were quickly on the scene and made a careful search for evidence of some new and less noisy variety of bomb, but the mystery was for the time being unsolved.

When daylight came a policeman took up the search, but never a fragment of clue, or trace of damage, could be found. Then a bright thought occurred to one of the householders. He remembered storing some home-made wine in the garage loft.

Sure enough, here was the origin of the sensation. Three of the bottles had gone off bang, bang, bang, and ears attuned to night alarms at once feared the worst !

" THEM SYRIANS ! "

(S.P.S.)

When the sirens first started to warn us of the approach of danger it was amusing to hear the various ways people pronounced this now familiar sound. Even now people talk about the " Syreens " just as they talk about the " I-talians." But there is one man I know who, from the first, *would* call them the " Syrians! " And, strangely enough, anyone who knows anything at all about the nature of this ancient race must agree that there is a certain appropriateness in his pronunciation, quaint though it is.

The tone emitted by our warning sirens was at first criticised by many people, but this is no longer the case. One such critic wrote to a local paper to say that though he at first criticised them, he wanted to express the real gratitude everybody now feels for the sirens. " We would like to say to those who render this service: ' Thank you, gentlemen for your watchful warnings, and whether it be Moan or Melody, Wail or Warble, carry on! ' "

" WHERE IS IT? "

(Mr. J. L. Greening, 18, Langham Road, Knowle.)

I was making my way during a blitz from Old Market to Victoria Street, along Temple Way, when a man came rushing out of a side street, shouting: " Where is it? Where is it?" He was carrying a stirrup-pump and was in a state of great excitement. Running towards Victoria Street, he was stopped by a policeman—one of those fine types of officer who are a credit to the Force. " What are you in such a hurry about?" he asked calmly. " Where is it? Where is it?" shouted the man. " Where's what?" asked the P.C. " That incendiary I saw falling," he explained, breathlessly. The officer smiled. " Just step along with me," he said, and led him to Victoria Street. " Look down there, my man." he chuckled. " There's a thousand just fallen along that street. Take your pump, and choose which one you like!"

That touch of humour *did* cheer me up. So typically English!

HELL CORNER

(Evening Post)

Drivers and members of First Aid Parties at a depot in Bristol were detailed to proceed to action stations some distance away during a blitz in December, 1940. When they arrived at a certain spot in the city they were at a loss to find their way.

On a corner which one last-war veteran described at " Hell Corner" they found a young man, aged about twenty, standing in the middle of the road directing traffic. Despite falling bombs and intense heat from the blazing houses on either side, he helped to guide the cars through, and was indirectly the means of saving the lives of many people in the area to which First Aid men were going. " He was a real hero," said one driver, " and all the men want to express their thanks to him." (But his name has never been revealed. Ed.).

SERMONS IN STONES

(Western Daily Press)

The thoughts of Bristolians in many parts of the world are turning more than ever to the old home town, for this, if ever, is her time of trial. Such thoughts have been well expressed by Mr. Cecil Watson, now living at Kirby, Cheshire, who was a school-boy at St. Mary Redcliffe, and Merchant Venturers. In spite of the passing of three-score-years and ten, his memory is very green.

He writes: " The Mint, the Old Temple, the Dutch House, where, out of a heap of fat cheroots, I bought my first cigar, my pipe and my tobacco. Would that I might, just for a moment, stand amidst the ruins and call down curses on those who harnessed science to destruction !

" Suffering as you are and brave as you well may be, those shrines of yours can never be rebuilt. You may replace them all, but rebuild? No! Not in a thousand years or over. You may place stone on stone, or build new and even lovlier structures, but you cannot rebuild them. The ghosts have gone !

" Strike and destroy St. Mary Redcliffe—which the Lord forbid— and the mystery and beauty of Chatterton has left you. The shades of Canynge and Penn would have vanished. No longer could we picture those venturing seamen keeping vigil, dedicating their souls to Almighty God, and sailing west to place a girdle round the earth, architects of our mighty Empire."

" HOLD THOU THY CROSS "

(S.P.S.)

During the days of frequent alerts a young lady came to see me about her banns. When this matter had been arranged, satisfactorily I hope, our conversation naturally turned to the subject which was foremost in our minds. We had been having some very bad nights, and I ventured to ask her what she did when the sirens sounded.

I shall never forget her quiet answer. " I just take hold of this," she said, indicating a little golden cross she was wearing, " then I feel that all will be well whatever happens."

BOMBED IN FOUR HOSPITALS

(H. DAVIES, 8, Wyedale Avenue, Coombe Dingle.)

In November, 1940, I was in Southmead Hospital when incendiaries dropped all round. Then the bombs came, and we just had to get under our beds. Then I went to the B.G.H. on January 3, 1941, to have an anæsthetic examination. While unconscious the sirens sounded, and when I came round I was being carried to the basement. I shall never forget that night. Children were crying and women moaning, but Matron, doctors and nurses were very brave, bringing round hot drinks for the patients. Opposite me was a man sitting up on a stretcher; he had eight nurses around him, and had them all singing: " I've got sixpence, jolly, jolly sixpence." All this time the roof was on fire and bombs were falling.

Then the order came through to move all patients to the B.R.I. I shall never forget that journey! When we arrived we were taken right to the top of the building; as one patient said—they must have thought we were the suicide squad! Jerry was still letting them fall, and every time we heard a bomb we had to dive under the bed. The next day we were all sent home, and I arrived in just an operating shirt and a pair of bedsocks. The same night incendiaries fell in our district—we had 21 fires in roofs and bedrooms in our street alone, and I went out to lend a hand. Next day I went for my clothes to the B.G.H., only to find that someone had lifted £5 10s. out of my pocket, leaving me a key and a shilling. I still have this as a keepsake. They also stole my diary.

Then I was sent to Weston-super-Mare for an operation, where I had the same nurse as at the B.G.H. (Nurse Pyle). While there Jerry visited us several times and gave us another shaking, as if we had not had enough. I left Weston in March only to run into the Good Friday blitz!

(The writer informs me that he has had 22 operations sinc 1918 and still enjoys the best of health!—Ed.).

GRANDFATHER CLOCK

(S. P. S.)

During the Sunday evening raid in November, 1940, a house opposite to our own in Brislington was burnt to the ground. Among the things salvaged was a grandfather clock which was placed for safety, along with many other things, in our garden. When morning dawned one of the members of my family had a shock when she saw two long bomb-shaped pieces of metal lying on the garden. A few hectic minutes followed—hasty attempts at explanation—decision to send for the A.R.P. But before they arrived all fears were quelled and calm, more or less, reigned in the curate's house. The two " infernal machines " turned out to be the weights of the grandfather's clock!

59

THE " B.G.H."

Anon.

No account of the raids on Bristol would be complete without a reference to the Bristol General Hospital and its Matron and Staff during two of the blitzes.

During the November (1940) raid the hospital had to deal with approximately 300 casualties, 100 of which were such serious cases that they had to be admitted to the wards.

On December 6th, heavy calibre bombs fell in close proximity; the blast from these bombs was so severe that practically all the windows in the hospital were shattered. There were 110 patients in the wards at the time, and their removal was rendered more difficult on account of the lifts not being available. The conditions prevailing in the hospital—no water, gas or electricity—were extremely trying,

" Removal from the wards was difficult."

but in spite of these handicaps the hospital continued to function efficiently.

On January 3rd, 1941, a large number of incendiaries were dropped on the building. The top floor was set alight, the nurses' and domestic servants' quarters were destroyed, and also four wards below. Several high explosives were also dropped close to the hospital which again suffered considerably from blast.

On both these occasions, and under the conditions prevailing immediately afterwards, the Matron, Miss Robins, and her entire staff, showed the utmost devotion to duty in the face of great danger. Miss Robins has since been awarded the O.B.E.—a tribute both to herself and her staff.

A MISCELLANY

A man with his new Sunday suit covered with mud and blackened with smoke, went home to his wife and explained that he had been rescuing neighbours from underneath their wrecked home.—*Evening World.*

A young married woman in the uniform of the ambulance service was visiting friends eight miles away when the alert sounded. She walked all the way home. "I must be on duty," she said, "for if I'm not there someone may die."—*Evening World.*

At the height of a blitz the people in a skittle alley shelter attached to a social centre were heard singing at the top of their voices. They stopped only when there was a call for volunteers to put out incendiaries which had fallen on the roof of the social centre itself.—*Evening World.*

The Recorder of Bridgwater had been conducting a service at the Colston Hall when the first blitz broke over the city. The people sat in their seats and sang for six hours, and then went home when the raid ended, unharmed. "We did not sing only hymns," said the Recorder afterwards. "We even sang, 'What shall we do with the drunken sailor'?"—*Evening World.*

A Bristol business man tells of an incendiary bomb which narrowly missed his office. It was recovered, and is now on the mantlepiece at his house. It bore the number 147—the number of his house!—*Evening Post.*

During the height of a blitz a car travelled, by devious routes, to the Suspension Bridge. As it drew up a toll collector came forward and put his usual query: "Single or return?" A fine example of "carrying on."—*Evening Post.*

"This is every bit as bad as Coventry," said Mrs. Churchill, when she was making a tour of some of the blitzed areas of Bristol. Her famous husband, who is not a man to wear his heart on his sleeve, was seen more than once to have tears rolling down his cheeks when some of the people who had lost everything ran to greet him.—*Evening Post.*

A man whose house was wrecked by a bomb which fell outside found four pieces of music on the blast-strewn piano when he went to the wreckage to hunt for his belongings. They were: "O Lovely Night," "Just For To-day," "Passing By," and "For You Alone."—*Evening World.*

Two wardens entered a lady's front garden to put out an incendiary. The door opened and a voice called out: "Mind my bulbs, please, won't you?" A fine example of morale!—*Evening World.*

Two elderly ladies always turned the knob of their wireless to crescendo when things were lively outside. The Luftwaffe couldn't terrify these stout-hearted old souls.—*Evening World.*

Two Sea Scouts helped to save a building by removing burning furniture and other goods. When asked for their names their reply was simply: "154th Sea Scouts, sir!"—*Evening World*.

When a bomb fell in a certain street it hurled an ash-can over a rank of houses and sent it crashing to earth in the next road. It was identified by amateurs as a petrol bomb, and was carefully roped off. It was some time before some knowledgable A.R.P. workers, to their great amusement, discovered the error.—*Western Daily Press*.

A cat which was buried for six days beneath the debris of a Bristol house was found to be unharmed and to have given birth to two kittens, both in a thriving condition. Puss was determined to give her youngsters a good start in life, for their bed was found to consist of a £1 and a 10/- note which had been blown out of a drawer.—*Western Daily Press*.

The oldest theatre in the country (the Theatre Royal), and the first to be State-supported, would have been completely destroyed but for the prompt action of a stage-hand, Mr. Felix Norris. He extinguished six incendiaries which crashed through the roof during the performance of a pantomime.—*Western Daily Press*.

" Better to be born lucky than rich," was the remark of a Special Constable after a remarkable escape. He had tossed a coin—" heads " for a shelter, " tails " for under the stairs. Heads won, and while in the shelter the constable was told his home had been demolished. —*Evening Post*.

A lady was describing to some friends the horrors of bombing. She illustrated her luried remarks by asserting that she saw at a certain bombed stores decaying limbs and parts of bodies among the debris. Probably she didn't know that at this particular store a number of artificial dummy figures and wax models were used!— *Western Daily Press*.

After-blitz optimism. A man stood in the City offering sprays of shamrock for sale on St. Patrick's Day, March 17th, 1941!— *Evening World*.

" I wish I'd been there to experience all that England is going through," writes a Bristol journalist, now in South Africa. " The millions of exiles abroad, like myself, will always feel they have been cheated of part of their destiny by not living in the land they love when her peril was greatest."—*Evening World*.

A Bristol man whose house was bombed, said to a reporter: " No, I don't want to be interviewed, but you can say I am proud to be a citizen of Blitzol!"—*Evening Post*.

A H.E. fell a dozen yards from a surface shelter in which there were nearly 150 people. " The shelter shook and a number of us were thrown out of our bunks, but that was all," was the quiet comment of a seventy-year-old lady.—*Evening Post*.

Letter from a little girl evacuee in a safe area: " It's so dull, mummy—no bombs and no sirens!"—*Evening World*.

"The fire-watchers were great," was the tribute of a hospital matron, where a detached building containing the nurses' quarters was set on fire, "and the fire brigade was marvellous. About 15 nurses who were on duty sheltered in a cellar; the others went on with their sewing in a room which contained eight bunks.—*Evening Post*.

The front door of a house which had gone up in flames remained in tact. On it read the official notice: "No Hawkers; No Circulars", to which someone added: "No Sightseers!"—*Evening Post*.

An aged gentleman, armed with a bucket of sand and a coal shovel, was putting out incendiaries right and left. He received a shock when one fell right into the bucket and fizzled out.—*Evening World*.

Two old ladies, both over 70, whose home was blitzed on March 16th, 1941, were bruised and shaken when dug out, but there was no word of complaint. On the way to hospital a H.E. dropped near the ambulance and rocked it violently. Still no complaints!— *Evening World*.

"We shall have plenty of fresh air now," said a woman to her neighbour. Her windows were completely smashed.—*Evening World*.

During one heavy raid a doctor sat all night by the side of a woman trapped in the basement of a house wrecked by a bomb, and from time to time administered anaesthetics.—*Evening World*.

"I'm not beaten yet," said Mrs. Hazen, aged 81, when the back of her house fell into the garden.—*Evening World*.

"While bombs were falling all around us," said an A.F.S. man, "a slip of a girl, about 18, with an 'A' on her tin hat, came coolly along and asked: 'Any casualties here?' I confess we were not feeling too happy about ourselves, but this girl was as cool as a cucumber."—*Evening World*.

Soldiers, acting as traffic controllers, had their own brand of humour. One was heard to say: "This way to Berlin; that way to Rome, madam!"—*Evening World*.

Another soldier, stationed at the top of High Street, kept the crowds moving by singing in a rich, tenor voice: "Keep moving, please, keep moving. There are no exceptions. Remember Felix! Remember Felix!"—*Evening World*.

Following the course of a bomb a Boy Scout hurried to the scene of wreckage, saw what had happened, rushed to a telephone and gave the call for a rescue party, then crawled through the debris, found the top of a cellar, and lay there comforting those below, until the rescue squad arrived and took out the survivors—and the others! —*Western Daily Press*.

A warden saved a grocer's shop from being gutted by an incendiary by putting his pick-axe through the ceiling and bringing down chunks of it on top of the fire.—*Evening Post*.

"Danger. No Lights. Gas Escaping," read a notice in one of the main streets of the city. A lorry driver and his mate, engaged on repair work, drove past, stopped, alighted, struck a light and lit their cigarettes. Let us hope this story had a happy ending. The one who related this story says he did not wait to see!—*Evening Post.*

Railway fire-fighters did fine work again and again. They risked H.E.s in order to save waggons, timber and warehouses. One of them led five horses to safety, and the same man, while attacking a mill fire later was machine-gunned; but he bravely carried on and rendered first-aid to an injured railwayman.—*Evening Post.*

A twelve-year-old girl, all dressed up for a New Year's party, put out eight fire bombs before setting off. Then she went to a doctor's surgery and settled another bomb. " It was great fun," she said, after a wash and brush up. She took the whole matter with great calmness, as though it were an everyday affair.—*Evening Post.*

SLOGANS OF THE BLITZ

Many citizens of Bristol showed their mettle by the slogans they displayed on their battered premises after the blitzes. This " Keep Your Chins Up " spirit helped to keep up the morale of the people in a wonderful way. Here are a few of them: —

A tailor displayed this notice on his wall: " Hitler suits nobody. I suit everybody."

A bakery and restaurant urged: " Hitler has paid us a visit. Why don't you?"

" No window cleaners wanted," read a notice in the window of a fruit shop in a busy Bristol street. The window was there, minus the glass!

Chalked on a lorry passing through Bristol: " If you can't be cheerful, shut up!"

Following the first blitz, Canon Swann, while walking along Redcliffe Street, noticed a wall which would need very little force to make it collapse. Some wag had chalked on it " Stick no bills."

" Business as Usual " appeared over many wrecked shops.

Notice in a partially wrecked barber's shop: " We Still Shave, Though We've Had a Close Shave."

Signs indicating where the owners of ruined premises have now moved are frequent. But one shop has gone better than this. The sign outside states that buses from across the road pass the new premises, and it is only a 1½d. fare!

Over an art shop: " Hitler may bomb our buildings but he can't bomb our souls."

Another cultural establishment displayed the well-known Latin tag: " Ars Longa, Vita Brevis."

Public house notice: " Our premises were damaged, but our beer is untouched. Beer is the best after-blitz tonic, and we have the best!"

Hand-written notice in window: " Stirup Pump Hear!"

PART III

HEROES OF THE BLITZ

A small boy once described a hero as " A bloke with plenty of guts and a chance to use 'em." That lad should grow up to be a philosopher, for he summed up in a homely phrase the essential characteristics of a hero. The second part of his definition was very important—" a chance to use 'em." Most people are really greater than they know. It only needs a challenging circumstance to arouse within them this dormant quality of valour. And when it is aroused the daring deed will probably be done with an unconscious spontaneity.

This, at any rate, was the opinion of that popular Victorian writer, Charlotte M. Yonge, whose biography has just been so well received by reviewers. In her " Book of Golden Deeds " she says: " If ever it be your lot to do a Golden Deed it will probably be in unconsciousness that you are doing anything extraordinary, and that the whole impulse will consist in the having absolutely forgotten self."

That is precisely what happened in our city during the blitzes. The moment of testing came, the crisis arrived, the unexpected happened—and brought out of thousands unsuspected heroic qualities.

Many stories have already been told about heroic actions during air raids on Bristol, and there will be many more to be told after the war is over.

A considerable number of Bristolians have been decorated for gallantry, among them being members of the Police and Civil Defence Services, of the National Fire Service and Hospital and Ambulance Services—in fact practically every Service has been honoured in some way and, in addition, many civilians have been amongst the recipients of gallantry awards. Servicemen, too, have distinguished themselves in assisting the civilian services during raids on the city.

TWICE DECORATED

One of the most unusual gallantry awards cases of this war is surely that of Mr. Henry Cox, of Bristol, 64-year-old member of a Rescue Squad.

Mr. Cox was awarded the British Empire Medal for the courage and enterprise he displayed on a night in November, 1940. A direct hit by a high explosive bomb had completely demolished a four-storeyed house at Kingsdown that night. When the Rescue Squad arrived there, the cries of a woman were heard coming from under the debris in the middle of the basement floor. As bombing was still going on, and the risk of falling debris was very great, it was going to be a difficult job to get to her. After a preliminary survey as to her position, Mr. Cox worked his way down through a small opening and found the poor woman buried up to her neck. A bucket was carefully lowered to him, and he proceeded to remove the rubble surrounding the woman with his bare hands, loading it into the bucket again and again. For an hour and a half he worked, all the time talking and singing to the trapped woman to keep up her spirits until at last he was able to lift her sufficiently clear to enable her to be rescued.

Then, in June, 1942, Mr. Cox's squad was sent to Weston-super-Mare, where a fierce air raid was in progress.

After a strenuous night's work they were called to an incident where a house had been demolished, leaving only the front wall standing. It was reported that five people were buried in the debris. Mr. Cox cut a hole in the floorboards only large enough to allow himself to squeeze through. If a larger hole had been cut, tons of masonry might have collapsed on the trapped people, three of whom were known to be in the front of the wreckage and two in the back. After reaching a young woman who died as he was trying to release her, Mr. Cox came to a boy who was buried lying on his back. He removed some of the debris around the boy with his hands and then, turning on his own back, proceeded to release the boy by catching hold of his hands and pulling both himself and the boy out by the use of his legs.

Another member of the squad, Mr. W. J. Tye, then took over to try to release a young girl whose legs were pinned between boxes which were taking the weight of some tons of debris above. This load of debris could not be moved without killing the two people trapped in the back of the wreckage as well as the little girl. It meant a long heart-breaking job to get her out gently.

The two men took it in turn to squeeze through the hole in the floorboards to try to release the poor child. As they worked they had to shield her body from loosened pieces of debris which kept falling down. A doctor was present, and he went down at intervals to administer morphia. Half-way through the operations he decided to amputate one of her legs, but Cox and Tye pleaded with him to give them a little longer. Eventually, after five hours, success crowned their efforts, and they were able to get her out safely.

The squad then went to the rescue of the two people who had been trapped in the back of the house, but when they reached them they found them dead.

For this wonderful piece of rescue work, Mr. Cox was awarded the George Medal, and Mr. Tye got the British Empire Medal.

The portrait of Mr. Henry Cox, G.M., B.E.M., has since been painted for the Nation's War Records, and it was recently shown as the Picture of the Month at the Bristol Art Gallery.

THE MOBILE CANTEEN

Typical of the spirit and enterprise of members of the Women's Voluntary Services has been the work of Mrs. F. C. W. Bamberger, who received the British Empire Medal in May, 1941.

Mrs. Bamberger used to drive a mobile canteen which she had presented to the Women's Voluntary Services. On every occasion when Bristol has been subjected to bombing she went to the scenes of the worst incidents in order to give the victims the comfort of a cup of tea and perhaps something to eat.

" The comfort of a cup of tea."

But her job did not finish there. When a raid was over she attended to the needs of the Rescue Squads and firemen who might be working at the scene of the damage.

On one occasion after a very severe raid she attended with her canteen for 17 days and nights in order to feed the people who had been made homeless and the soldiers who had been called in to demolish certain unsafe buildings.

Her job was often very dangerous, and the arrival of her canteen at moments of heavy raiding has on many occasions been greeted by cheers from the Rescue Squads and other helpers who have previously had experience of her good service. Even when electricity, gas and water supplies were interrupted, Mrs. Bamberger still managed to produce tea and to serve it up with a smile.

One of her most exciting nights was on the occasion of the fourth blitz on Bristol. At the beginning of the raid she was in a building which received a direct hit. Luckily she was unhurt, so she started bandaging some of the wounded people and then helped to fight the fires which soon broke out.

Afterwards, she went with her schoolboy son to get out her canteen and, in doing so, had a very narrow escape from a bomb which exploded close by. The roads were thick with ice that night, but, undaunted, Mrs. Bamberger reported to her headquarters and was sent with her canteen to another part of the city. She remained there until 9.30 next morning, returning only to replenish her supplies and go out again to feed the fire squads who were still attending fires in certain parts of the city.

Mrs. Bamberger is only one of the many gallant women who answer the call of duty when the siren wails. She and many others like her have been a source of comfort to countless people when their spirits have been low as the result of bombing and all it leaves behind.

HE TOOK OUT THE GRATE

Another George Medallist whose portrait has been painted for the Nation's War Records is Mr. Herbert Stanford, a Group Warden who, in November, 1940, was instrumental in saving the lives of several people who had been trapped in a bombed house near Redcliff Hill.

While wardens were evacuating the residents of adjacent houses, cries were heard coming from beneath the blazing debris. Mr. Stanford investigated and came to the conclusion that some people were trapped under the demolished building and were alive. A fire pump was quickly brought to the scene, and while water was being played on the fire, Mr. Stanford worked his way through to the victims on his stomach and was able to give them some water while he spoke encouragingly to them.

It was found impossible to get the trapped people out alive by removing the debris on top, and so it was decided to make a hole in the wall which divided the shattered building from the next house. Unfortunately, however, when this had been done it was found still impossible to get through as there was an obstruction by debris inside, and there was a temporary hold-up. Mr. Stanford, however, was not to be beaten and decided a way could be cleared by knocking out a fire grate. This was an awkward task but it was achieved and it was effective; access was obtained and five people were brought out and taken to hospital. All this took three hours to accomplish—three hours during which the building was still burning, coal gas was escaping, and the raid was still going on.

DANGER—UNEXPLODED BOMB

Everyone remembers the delayed action bomb menace. Apart from the danger of these bombs, how annoying it was to be kept out of one's home or office because a delayed action bomb had fallen in the street, and even deviations to avoid them became irksome.

The Bomb Disposal officials were very over-worked in those days. Mr. C. D. Bruce, of the A.R.P. Communication Service offered to undertake the dangerous work of examining and reporting on unexploded bombs in the Bristol area. Many of these delayed action bombs were dropped in the latter part of 1940, and Mr. Bruce dealt with hundreds of them. He had some narrow escapes in doing so, particularly after a heavy raid, where a large number of unexploded bombs were found. For the courage he displayed in voluntarily undertaking this highly dangerous work Mr. Bruce was awarded the George Medal.

PATCHING THE GASHOLDER

It is pretty certain that most people have thought at one time or another during an air raid: "Will they get the gasholder this time?"

During a heavy raid on Bristol in November, 1940, two incendiary bombs fell on the top of the gasholder at St. Philip's. Without hesitation, Mr. G. D. Jones, the gasholder attendant, climbed the 70 feet to the top, and knocked the bombs off with his steel helmet before they had burnt through the plates of the holder. He was aware at the time that the holder contained over 2 million cubic feet of gas.

During the same raid the holder was punctured several times by pieces of bomb splinter and flying shrapnel. Each time he heard the sound of escaping gas, and although the raid was at its fiercest, Mr. Jones climbed up and stopped the holes with clay, thereby averting the danger of fire.

On another occasion, the gasholder was badly punctured and caught fire. Although Mr. Jones was not on duty that night he immediately went to the scene of the fire, and it was chiefly due to his efforts that it was put out before any serious damage was done.

For his high qualities of courage and devotion to duty Mr. Jones was awarded the George Medal in May, 1941.

BLITZ BABY

Another interesting story is that of two Sisters from the Bristol Maternity Hospital, Elsie Stevens and Violet Frampton. These two courageous women were each awarded the George Medal for the work they did during a severe raid on the city in March, 1941.

Shortly after the alert sounded that night, a call was received at the hospital requesting assistance for a woman about to have a baby. Sisters Stevens and Frampton immediately volunteered to go out, and found their journey a perilous one; bombs were falling and dislodged masonry added to the risks of passage through the streets. On arrival at their destination, they found that their patient was trapped with several other people in the cellar of a house which was in a very dangerous condition. In fact, circumstances were so bad, the raid being at its height, that it had been found practically impossible to continue rescue operations.

Sister Stevens was lowered through a narrow opening, actually a grating, and by lying flat was able to reach one victim. Her difficulties were increased by the fact that the only light available was that given by a torch. However, with the assistance of Sister Frampton and the Rescue Party, an old lady and two children were released and passed through the grating to safety.

As the pregnant woman was found to be completely buried under debris, Sister Frampton went back to the Hospital to obtain morphia. When she returned, Sister Stevens was again lowered into the cellar in order to give the patient an injection. By that time conditions were so dangerous that rescue work overhead had to be suspended. There was all the time grave risk of the whole building collapsing owing to blast and the shaking of the debris. Nevertheless, the two Sisters went down again and stayed beside their patient, and by 3 a.m. they had managed to release her head. They were then able to make her more comfortable, and sustained her with sips of warm tea. All through the night they remained with her while the Rescue Party worked to clear a way out.

At about 8 o'clock it was thought necessary to call a doctor. He answered the call immediately and went down into the cellar, staying with the Sisters, all three of them doing what they could for the patient in the very awkward and dangerous circumstances until they were finally released at 1 o'clock in the afternoon, when the patient was taken to hospital. Soon afterwards it was known that mother and child were doing well.

AMBULANCE ATTENDANT

The emancipation of women is surely now complete. During raids we find operating not only the better-known women's services, but also women ambulance drivers and attendants, women wardens and fireguards, and just women. In fact, women seem to be working side-by-side with the men in every way in this war except in the actual fighting itself.

Mrs. Violet Olive is an Ambulance Attendant with the Bristol Casualty Services.

During a raid one Sunday night in 1940, she was attending to a patient who was lying on the ground when a bomb fell nearby. As she heard the whistle of the bomb, Mrs. Olive threw herself over her patient, and in doing so was injured in the back by a falling door. Needless to say, had the door fallen on the patient the shock might well have proved fatal.

Although the blow was so severe that Mrs. Olive had to have her back set in plaster for some considerable time afterwards, she continued to work all through that night and, in addition, she reported for duty regularly throughout the following week.

Some time later she received an expression of Commendation from His Majesty the King.

THE UNKNOWN HERO

Only a few stories of gallantry are quoted here, out of the large number, perhaps a century, which received publicity and a formal award. They are, however, typical of the Bristolian in action—of his stamina, of his courage, and of his practical resourcefulness.

The published stories, again, are only a small proportion of those which have been told by observers, by assistants, and by the grateful recipients, of self-sacrificing service in nerve-racking and arduous hours of peril. Some of these have been elbowed aside by more startling events; others have failed to secure official recognition only for lack of enough independent evidence. They were no less deserving.

And in the background remains the mass of anonymous service, steadfast and unselfconscious, which Bristolians of all ages and of both sexes have rendered to their fellow-citizens and to the wartime and passing visitors to their historic city.

The scars of war will heal and fade from memory, but the spirit of the " South Western Town," tried in the vintage years of 1939-1941 and never daunted, will not be forgotten, here or at the ends of the earth.

RESILIENCE

I stood on the brow of a smouldering hill,
  And gazed on a city a thousand years old;
It lay at my feet in an ocean of fire,
  Writhing in agony, tested as gold

In a furnace. Her churches 'midst torturing flames
  Stood guarding, like sentinels, her proud, unbow'd soul,
Symbols of things which naught can destroy—
  Love, mercy, truth, justice; Man's faith in his goal.

S. P. S.